LIVE THE LIFE YOU WANT WITH THE MONEY YOU HAVE

THE MONEY HANDBOOK FOR A NEW GENERATION

VINCE SCULLY

MAJOR
STREET

MAJOR STREET First published in 2022 by Major Street Publishing Pty Ltd
info@majorstreet.com.au | +61 421 707 983 | majorstreet.com.au

 A catalogue record for this book is available
from the National Library of Australia

Printed book ISBN: 978-1-922611-34-5
Ebook ISBN: 978-1-922611-35-2

Cover design by Typography Studio
Internal design by Production Works
Printed in Australia by IVE Group, an Accredited ISO AS/NZS 14001:2004
Environmental Management System Printer.

10 9 8 7 6 5 4 3 2 1

Disclaimer

This book was written as a handbook for a new generation of Australians – generally those born after the oil shocks of the mid-1970s, who are now in their 20s, 30s or 40s. This means the content cannot take into account the specific needs or financial objectives of any individual reader and so cannot constitute specific commercial, financial, investment, accounting, taxation or legal advice.

Before making any financial decisions, you should consider whether the content is appropriate in your individual circumstances and seek advice from a qualified professional. In particular, before deciding to acquire a financial product, read the relevant disclosure document and consider whether the product is suitable for your needs, objectives and circumstances.

Vince Scully is a representative of MoneySherpa Pty Ltd, which holds Australian Financial Services Licence #451289 and Australian Credit Licence #451289 issued by the Australian Securities and Investments Commission.

Contents

Preface

'There is no dignity quite so impressive, and no one independence quite so important, as living within your means.'
– Calvin Coolidge, former US President (1923–1929)

Whenever I tell people what I do for a living – I'm a financial planner at Life Sherpa® (trademark owned by Moneysherpa Pty Ltd), Australia's first online financial planner – the conversation inevitably turns to money. I may be at a barbeque or even out for a run or a cycle when people ask me what they should do with their money: what should they invest in? What should they do about tax?

My first response is always, 'It depends', because unfortunately, there is no one right answer. But I can give you a process to lead you to your right answer simply, without needing a degree in finance or a bunch of spreadsheets. Luckily, most of it is about behaviour and attitude, not complex mathematics and technical finance stuff.

Let me explain. Over the many years I've worked in finance, I have discovered that successfully navigating the world of money is not about having the best plan, or choosing the best investment, or even earning the most money. Nor is it about scrimping and saving – the money equivalent of the crash diet. I realised that the less time we spend planning how to get the most from our money, the more time we spend worrying about it.

I have worked with clients just starting out who have very little money and lots of debt. I have also worked with clients who have millions of dollars in retirement savings. And what made them comfortable with their money, and allowed them to get the most life out of their money, was not how much they earned or saved or where they invested it. What made the difference was truly understanding what they wanted and spending their money in a way that got them closer to achieving that objective. These weren't money goals like 'I need to pay off so much debt' or 'I need to save so much for retirement'. They were true life goals and values.

Over time, I developed a system that helped my clients understand their core values – what truly mattered to them – and use this information to develop a life plan – or at least one for the next few years! We then worked together to develop a spending plan, and to build the money skills needed to get there.

Like a lot of people, I learned a lot about money from my father. But I also know the world has changed since he started out. What got him to a fulfilling life and a comfortable retirement isn't the same thing that will get me there, and it certainly isn't going to work for you if you are just starting out.

This insight, informed by years of practice as a financial planner, led me to launch Life Sherpa. And by writing this book, I can provide you with some simple, practical tools to get the most out of the money you have. This book will help you develop an understanding of what really matters to you and give you an easy-to-follow, eight-step plan to help achieve it. I'm not going to harangue you about the things you spend your money on. I'm certainly not going to tell you to cut out your morning coffee. But I will give you the skills to live a fulfilling life free of money stress, no matter how much you earn, own or owe.

The eight-step roadmap to financial freedom is a program I developed and is now used by my team at Life Sherpa. Thousands of our members have used it over the years, so we know it is a system that anyone can use to stop getting by and start getting ahead. Each step will bring you closer to financial freedom.

There are three foundation steps, setting you right on the road to success: spend less than you earn, build an emergency stash, and pay off your debts. Then there are three protective steps, keeping the unexpected from throwing you off: prepare for the unexpected, get the superannuation (super) basics right, and get your paperwork straight. And finally, there are two growth steps, the bits that give you that powerful sense of getting ahead: buy and pay off your home, and invest your surplus.

Have you ever thought:

- 'I make a good living; how come I don't have anything to show for it?'
- 'If one more person tells me that if I just cut out my morning coffee or took my lunch to work, I could afford a house or to retire rich…'?
- 'I struggle from payday to payday, but there never seems to be anything left over'?
- 'I'll never be able to afford a house of my own'?
- 'Retirement seems so far away; I just can't think about my super'?
- 'Money is just too complicated; I can't make a decision'?
- 'Why does this money stuff all have to be such hard work?'
- 'I'm only 30; do I really need to think about all this stuff right now?'
- 'Who can I really trust to help me with my money?'

Then this book is for you.

The latte fallacy

There is a commonly held but incorrect view that giving up your morning coffee can make you rich. At just $3.80, your daily latte will cost you $83,023 over 30 years, and that's why millennials can't afford a house. Sounds plausible, right?

The maths seems straightforward enough at first blush: $3.80 a day times 365 days a year is $1387 in the first year and $41,610 over 30 years. Of course, inflation will increase the cost of your daily latte each year, so the actual cost over 30 years would be $65,987 (at 3% annual inflation). If instead you invested this at 5% after tax you would end up with $134,681 at the end of 30 years.

The notion that how much you spend on coffee is the difference between success in life and a retirement spent in penury has strong currency in the media and among personal finance bloggers. So how could it be so wrong on so many levels?

The maths is flawed. It ignores the fact that the $134,681 is only worth $57,151 in today's money after 30 years when you adjust for inflation. And it's the same maths that says your daily latte, which contains 176 calories, will result in you putting on eight kilograms a year, or 240 kilograms over 30 years.

This is a game economists love to play – it's called keeping everything else constant. And this is simply not realistic when it comes to human behaviour, and especially when it comes to money behaviour. The truth is that most people spend most of their money most of the time. This explains why couples without children do not accumulate more assets than couples with children, despite the obvious cost of raising children.

It's simply not true that millennials are actually squandering their hard-earned. We may spend 50% more on eating out than we did 40 years ago, but the total amount we spend on food adjusted for inflation has not materially changed since the mid-1980s. And why pick on coffee? We spend nine times as much on alcohol as we do on coffee, so why isn't alcohol blamed for millennials not being able to afford a home?

Why is this message such a problem? Isn't this just a harmless metaphor – a modern take on your grandmother's advice that you should look after the pennies and the pounds will take care of themselves? Perhaps the metaphor is not intended to be taken literally, but this money meme is not just harmless fun – it is leading to bad money management for most Australians. It focuses the mind on cutting small, highly visible expenses, rather than the big ones that actually make a real difference. This makes managing your spending harder work than it needs to be.

The truth is that success with money is not the result of thousands of small decisions made well – it's a function of half a dozen decisions made with intention and consideration: where you live, what you drive, how you prepare for the unexpected, how you prepare for retirement, how you make a living, and who you marry.

For example, the difference between spending $735,000 and $700,000 on your home will pay for a lifetime of lattes – invested in a balanced fund, that $35,000 should generate an income of $1400 (indexed to inflation) with a high degree of certainty. Yet when we go to inspect real estate, the agent is likely to say something like, 'This will sell in the low seven hundreds'. This is agent code for $700,000 to $750,000 – as if these were so close that it made no real difference.

I don't mean to say you shouldn't control your spending; far from it. Spending less than you earn is the foundation of financial success. In this book I'll show you lots of ways to do that and still feel free to enjoy life. I call this the art of living the life you want with the money you have.

The world has changed

The world has changed massively since your parents' and grandparents' time, so many of the money rules need to change too. Old rules – such as 'Buy the biggest house you can afford, even if you have to stretch yourself a bit at the beginning', or 'If only you spent less on coffee/ going out/clothes/[insert other pleasure here], you would be fine' – simply don't work in today's world.

This is not to say that your parents or grandparents are wrong or misguided. It's just that the game has changed, and so the way we play it needs to change, too. This means that much of what passes for common sense doesn't actually make sense anymore, so I want to share the new rules and how you can make them work for you.

What has changed to make life today so different to your parents' world?

Banking has changed, for one thing. When your parents or grandparents were young, you could be pretty sure that if you had a good steady job and lived a normal life, you could afford a nice house and a car, and money sort of took care of itself. This is not because your parents were any better at managing money. It's just that the system wouldn't let them spend more than they earned. When their pay packet was spent, they had to stop spending until the next one

3

arrived. The government regulated the activities of the banks so you could only borrow what you could really afford to pay back, and credit cards were rare. This made it pretty hard to overcommit on debt repayments and let your finances get out of balance.

Now, Australians owe a collective $17.9 billion on 13.2 million cards. I'm certainly not advocating a return to such government regulation, but it is important to understand what has changed to create the need for a new set of rules.

Also, inflation has been tamed. Back when inflation was high, it didn't really matter too much if you were a bit stretched when you bought your home, or you paid a little too much for it, or you borrowed a little more than you could really afford. Inflation came along and delivered pay rises and home price increases, and soothing relief for the previously overstretched borrower.

To see what I mean, let's go back to 1979, when the median house price in Sydney was $50,700, average (male) earnings were $12,896, inflation was running at 10.2% and home loan rates were at 9.13%. Our first homebuyer who borrowed $40,000 to buy this $50,700 median house would face payments of $4,475 per year or 35% of their pay. (As you will learn in Step 1, this is an uncomfortably large percentage.) Within a year, their pay rise (to $14,456) would reduce it to 31%, and by December 1981, it would be down to a comfortable 28%. Meanwhile, the value of the house has increased to $68,850 in a year and to $78,900 by December 1981. So even if they paid a few thousand more than the house was really worth, it has now become almost academic.

Roll forward to 2021: inflation is down to less than 3%, home loan rates are around 2% and wages growth is barely keeping up with inflation. The impact on your lifestyle of stretching your budget to buy that first home will now last for much longer.

Despite the apparent huge increase in the cost of housing in Australia, the proportion of the average household budget spent on housing costs has changed little in the past few decades. How is this possible? For starters, the typical household now has two earners, and women are earning more than before. So, as household income has risen, we have typically spent the same portion of it on housing. (This is a recurring theme we will come back to – I call it lifestyle inflation, and it can be damaging.)

Also, interest rates have fallen. When interest rates fell from 10% to 5%, the amount you could borrow for any given monthly payment rose by 63%, and the fall of interest rates to 2% increased it by a further 45%. And lending terms have eased, with the term of a home loan increasing from 20 years to 30 or more. Increasing the term from 20 years to 30 years allows you to borrow 35% more with the same monthly payment. These factors explain much of the rise in house prices over the past few decades.

Another way the world has changed is that we have to do more for ourselves. When our parents or grandparents started work, it was common to have a job for life, and a company provided a pension based on how much they earned. For others, there was always the age pension. However, when compulsory super was introduced in 1992, we were all effectively turned into mini pension fund managers, a task for which we were (and still are) generally ill-equipped. We now make a number of financial decisions every week that, cumulatively, have huge impacts on the overall outcome, but we haven't really been given the tools or education to cope with this. Nor has affordable financial advice been available for the vast majority of Australians.

The good news is that anyone who entered the workforce after 2002 should be capable of retiring on about 60% of their pre-retirement income from their super contributions, given a bit of focus and the right advice.

Society today is also more socially mobile than in our parents' or grandparents' days. This means we are exposed to people with vastly different levels of income and wealth than our own. We see people with much less than we have, and we see people with much more. Because money is the last taboo – we are happier to talk about sex than money – it can be difficult to assess from the outside how others really compare to us. Comparisons can be dangerous. Just because your neighbour has a fancy German car doesn't mean you can afford it, too. You never know how much debt they have built up or whether they have other sources of income.

Our parents generally only saw such lifestyles on television or at the movies, where it was easier to tell fantasy and reality apart. Your neighbour might be living a debt-fuelled fantasy. Facebook and Instagram are a particularly pernicious influence here. We portray our lives on Facebook as we wish them to be seen. These carefully curated lives can provide a warped sense of reality that makes comparisons especially dangerous. As Steve Jobs said, 'Your time is limited, so don't waste it living someone else's life'.

We are also now spending longer in education and deferring life events like marriage, starting a family and buying a home. In 1990, the median age for first marriages was 26.5 years for men and 24.3 years for women; by 2019 this had increased to 30.7 years and 29.3 years, respectively. Between 1990 and 2020, the proportion of Australians aged 24 to 65 with a bachelor's degree rose from 10% to 39%. The average age of first homebuyers has risen from 25 in the 1970s to 35 in 2020. Almost a quarter of first-time mums are now over 35.

In contrast, we don't seem to be prepared to accept that 75 should be the new 65, so we should work until we are older to offset the later start. There has been only a small change in the age at which we retire. Of those who have already retired, 75% did so by age 65. Retirement intentions show that 34% intend to retire by 65, with 83% intending to retire by 69. But we are also living longer. As a result, we are working for a smaller proportion of our lives and expecting to live a longer, more active retirement. One of our biggest challenges is to make 40 years of income pay for 70 years of adult life. Something has to give!

As we have become more prosperous, our options have multiplied. Some choice is always beneficial; too much can become a burden. Faced with a complex decision, many of us simply give up and do nothing. In many parts of our lives, this is harmless, but when it comes to our finances it can be disastrous.

A study by psychologists Mark Lepper and Sheena Iyengar demonstrated this reluctance to make a decision when overwhelmed with choice. In the study, researchers set up displays featuring a range of jams, where customers could taste samples and receive a coupon for a dollar off if they bought a jar. One test had six varieties of the jam. Another had 24 varieties. The larger range of jams attracted more people to the table than the smaller range. In both tests, people tasted about the same number of jams. But when it came to buying, there was a huge difference: 30% of the people exposed to the small range of jams bought a jar, while only 3% of those exposed to the large range of jams made a purchase.

When I read this research, I thought it was nonsense. But when faced with the need to buy a new toaster, I found myself turning tail from a department store when faced with a choice of more than 30 toasters. I returned a few days later to buy the cheapest one!

All these changes mean we need new rules to live by. The human brain evolved to deal with clear and immediate threats, such as hunting lunch or escaping a rampaging woolly mammoth. But it doesn't do so well when faced with great complexity coupled with uncertainty – which describes many of the decisions we need to make in our financial lives. Fortunately, we also have the ability to develop and use shortcuts to create a practical way that may not be guaranteed to be optimal or perfect, but is sufficient for the immediate goals. Psychologists call these heuristics.

In this book, I include a number of rules of thumb that can help cut through the noise and allow you to quickly answer questions such as: how much house can I afford? What car should I drive? Can I afford to take time off when I have a child? What school should I send my child to? How much should I save for retirement? And how much is enough?

The important conclusion to take from this is that you can't win today's money game playing by yesterday's money rules. In this book, I share with you these new rules.

Why should I care in my 20s and 30s?

It is tempting to treat our 20s as a period of extended downtime between university and life: a period of travel and experimentation, punctuated by the occasional low-engagement job, and a time to defer life's responsibilities. I'm not suggesting that this is not a good time to enjoy new-found freedoms and to sample as many experiences as possible. But just as a building is only as good as its foundations, the rest of your life is critically dependent on the experiences, discoveries and activities of your 20s. Build them wisely!

As a society we may be settling down, marrying, buying a home and having children later than our parents and grandparents, but that doesn't mean that our brains and bodies have adapted accordingly. While our bodies might be maturing earlier now, our new lifestyles may be delaying the development of the very mental skills needed to survive and thrive in the 21st century. With the rise of the 'kidult', the extended adolescence supported by living with our parents longer has been shown to delay the development of the critical thought processes we need to make our way in the world.

Also, our brains develop a little later. In fact, the frontal lobe – the bit that deals with rational decision making in emotional or uncertain situations – is the last part to develop. It doesn't really come into play until we are well into our 20s. This development explains much of the reckless behaviour exhibited by young men in particular. When faced with emotional decisions or extreme uncertainty, teenagers and young adults are simply not yet equipped to think things through using rational processes.

Researchers now believe that, like muscle development, our brain functions benefit from use. Practice does in fact make perfect. These skills don't come just with age; they come with practice and experience. In other words, what we do in our 20s lays the foundations for how we deal with the rest of our lives.

When we look back over our lives, much of what shapes us as people and the way we live happens in our early adult life. Psychologists call these events and memories 'autobiographically consequential experiences'. These are the events we remember as having affected the unfolding of our life stories in personally significant ways, not merely events that affected the location we ended up, the jobs we took or the people with whom we connected. Simply put, our lives are largely defined by the experiences of our university and early adult years.

This is also true in our work lives. As much as the defining attribute of work in the 21st century is the portfolio career and the growth of the 'slashie' – as in actor/barista or accountant/novelist – some things haven't really changed. Our earning power still peaks in our early 40s and is hugely affected by experience gained in our 20s. In general, wages rise strongly through our 20s as each year of experience adds more value to an employer. As we grow into our 30s, we seem willing to give more to prospective employers. In our 40s, we are seen as more expensive and less open to change, as well as more focused on family and less on work. And by our 50s, many are starting to use their greater financial resilience to experience more fulfilling but perhaps less remunerative work. By building our skills, experience and networks in our 20s, we build the foundation of success through our 30s and 40s.

As for our social lives, most of our closest friends are made in our school and university days. Moving jobs and cities brings us into contact with many more people and widens our social circles.

Where we choose to live is determined in part by where our social circle lives, but it in turn changes or reinforces who joins or remains in our social circle.

Where we live and the people we socialise with have a huge impact on our cost of living. What's more, we tend not to move very far once we choose a city. In Sydney, for example, it is highly unusual for someone to move from the north shore to the eastern suburbs, or vice versa. We also tend to unconsciously conform to the lifestyles of our friends and neighbours. We live in similar houses, we drive similar cars, our kids socialise together, and they go to the same schools. These are the big four when it comes to spending. In other words, our budget is strongly influenced by the home we choose and the friends we keep. I'm not suggesting it is simply preordained; rather, I am saying that it takes more mental effort to be different.

In his 1955 article in *The Economist*, Cyril Northcote Parkinson, a British naval historian and author, wrote about how 'work expands so as to fill the time available for its completion'. This law can be expressed more generally as follows: the demand for a resource tends to expand to match the supply of the resource. So it is with money. Left unchecked, our spending grows to just exceed our income.

You would think that for something as basic as food, we would all spend roughly the same amount. After all, we all need to consume roughly the same number of calories to survive and, generally, rich people don't seem to be fatter than poor people. In fact, the opposite seems to be true: poorer people tend to suffer from greater levels of obesity. In practice, however, households across the income spectrum in Australia (and elsewhere) tend to spend the same proportion of their income on food – about 10%. As we get wealthier, there is a quality substitution effect: we stop eating cheap, processed foods and eat more fresh and organic foods.

We see the same effect with housing. Australian households spend roughly the same proportion of their budget on housing regardless of income. So as our income increases, we develop spending habits to match. We buy a bigger house, we drive a more expensive car, we take more expensive holidays, send our kids to more expensive schools, drink better wine and eat better food. The great difficulty occurs when our income later falls – it is so much more difficult to change a spending habit than to have never had it in the first place.

So, our 20s are the perfect time to head off the effects of lifestyle inflation. It is easy to get carried away with the flush feeling that comes from our first pay packet from our first real job. Freed from the deprivations of a student budget, we now have a sense of wealth and a feeling that we need to reward ourselves for the years of hard work. Go ahead, celebrate the wins, but be careful of building in structural spending that becomes hard to shift later.

It can also be tempting, particularly for people in creative or professional positions, to seek to look the part of the successful young employee. This means the right clothes, restaurants, bars, car and apartment. In many cases, living the perception of the right lifestyle costs a lot more than the reality of the pay packet.

Careers with a defined growth path – accounting and law in particular – can often deliver a steady stream of pay rises as you progress from graduate trainee to senior, to manager and, eventually, to partner. This can lead to a dangerous feeling of complacency – spending next year's pay rise this year. If you continue down the career path smoothly and happily, time will fix the problem (eventually). But you need to be very sure it is the career for you. Over the years, I have seen many clients who have built the lifestyle to match the 'successful lawyer' career only to find they are trapped in a job they hate because they can't afford to leave. I have lost track of the number of people I've met with seemingly successful careers and lavish lifestyles who wake up on their 25th birthday (or their 30th, 40th or 50th) and wonder if that's really all there is to it.

Building a balanced budget in line with your career stage, values and ambitions is the key to staving off the worst effects of lifestyle inflation.

Change after 30 is harder. There is a phrase often associated with the Jesuits, an order of Catholic priests, that emphasises the importance of early education in our future development: 'Give me the child for his first seven years, and I'll give you the man'. Whether seven is the right number is open to debate, but it is certainly true that we become who we are at an early age. The older we get, the less likely we are to change, as it is much harder to unlearn old habits and form new ones.

Recent analysis of Spotify listener data showed that as users grow out of their teens and enter their 20s, they listen to less popular music and more music with fewer listeners. This decline in the proportion of popular music continues until their early 30s when, for the average listener, their tastes have matured and the decline slows or stops – they are who they're going to be.

Thirty seems to be an important breakpoint. This is not to suggest that the morning of our 30th birthday is somehow different to the evening before, although many do wake up feeling that life is beginning to leave them behind. The Germans have a word for this – *torschlusspanik* – which literally means the fear that the gate is about to close. It is more commonly applied to a 40-something midlife crisis, but it can be experienced at any age.

At 20, your life lies ahead of you. Your biggest asset is time. Time is capable of curing many problems, and this is most true when it comes to money.

There is an old saying (often dubiously attributed to Einstein) that, 'Compound interest is the eighth wonder of the world. He who understands it, earns it … he who doesn't … pays it'. If you invest at 10% for five years, your money will grow to be worth 1.6 times its original value. If you invest at that rate for 50 years – ten times as long – your money will not grow by 16 times but will be worth more than 117 times its original value. This is a concept that many struggle to understand, but which is vital to understanding how to win with money.

What's that got to do with 20-something you? In practice, it means that the earlier you start saving, the more interest you earn, and the less you have to give up today to achieve the same future goal. Compare three savers: the first starts saving $2500 a year at 21 years of age and stops at 30, putting a total of $25,000 into savings; the second saver starts at 31 and contributes $2500 a year until the age of 70, for a total of $100,000; and the third starts at birth, when her parents put $2500 aside for two years, for a total of $5000. Each of these savers would end up with roughly $550,000 at age 70.

It's not just about saving for retirement. The effect extends to all forms of spending and saving. A dollar saved early is worth more than one saved late, and a dollar borrowed early ends up costing more. The earlier you start with balanced spending habits, the greater the beneficial effect. Each extra dollar saved for your new car, or your deposit on your flat, or paid off your home loan, or saved by better allocating your spending, has a similar effect. Harnessing this is the key to success.

Understanding yourself

The first step to achieving peace with your money is to get a firm grip on what is really important to you. The concept of understanding your deep inner values may seem a little out of place in a book about money; it may seem a little new age, but stay with me.

In his 2009 book *Start With Why*, Simon Sinek wrote, 'It doesn't matter what you do, it matters why you do it'. Similarly, Roy

Disney – Walt's nephew, who is famous for making some tough decisions at Disney, including ousting two CEOs – said, 'It's not hard to make decisions when you know what your values are'. And Stephen Covey, author of *The 7 Habits of Highly Effective People*, said, 'It's easy to say "no!" when there's a deeper "yes!" burning inside'.

What these guys are all saying is that when you understand the things that really matter to you (your core values), it's easier to conceive the right plan and to stick to it. Kate Moss, the famous model who was a poster girl for the heroin chic look, put it even more simply: 'You've got to want to be skinny more than you want chocolate cake'.

Midlife crises are often a result of living a life out of step with core values. It's hard to imagine that someone could turn 50 and suddenly say, 'I've lived true to my values, but now I don't like those values anymore, so I think I'll get divorced and start over'.

So, what is it about these values that make them so intrinsic to a fulfilling life? We all have a handful of values that define how we view the world and our place in it. Values are not New Year's resolutions, goals or to-do lists. Goals are about doing and having. Values are about being. You probably know what your values are, or what you value most in this life, even if you can't quite name them. They aren't necessarily constants; they evolve over time. You're not likely to see radical changes, but the relative importance of each will grow and change with you.

I'd like you to set aside some quality time to identify your core values and bring them to your conscious mind. Don't rush it. Find a quiet space with no interruptions. Depending on your personality type, you might find it more effective to do this with a friend.

Start by listing the values that seem important to you. Don't obsess too much. Go with your gut and write them down. There are no silly answers. Be frank and, most importantly, don't judge yourself, your answers or your partner's answers. Everyone is different, so don't feel the need to have the same values as your partner or neighbour. Here is a list of common values compiled by the Centre for Ethical Leadership, plus a few others, to help get you started. Don't worry if yours aren't here. This list is just to inspire you and get the ball rolling on your values:

peace	love	fame
truth	status	integrity
success	wealth	influence
recognition	authenticity	justice
joy	friendship	wisdom
happiness	family	power
security	health	creativity
excitement	freedom	making a difference
adventure	growth	spirituality
peace of mind	fulfilment	balance
fun	independence	confidence

Now look for some common themes in your list of values. Group or eliminate these. For example, you may have identified adventure and excitement. Are these different to you? If so, keep both. If they both express the same core value for you, keep the one that best resonates, or find a word that expresses both. Refine your list to leave only five or six values that really resonate.

Think of some life experiences and how you felt or reacted. This will help you distil your list. Here are some examples:

· Think of a day or time that you consider the best of your life.
· What do you remember about your childhood?
· What would you like people to say about you at your funeral? What would you say about yourself if you could give a farewell speech?

- Why do you get out of bed in the morning? Why do you go to work? Why do you want to make money? Keep following this train of thought until you hit on something with deep intrinsic meaning.
- How do you fill the space around you? How do you spend your money, your time and your energy? What stands out as the most valuable to you emotionally?
- Think of times when you are most focused, energised, organised and ready for anything.
- What do you talk to yourself about? What themes, events, desires and concerns occupy your mind each day? What themes come up often when you talk to others? These are clues as to what you value.

Once you have completed this task, you should have a list of five values that are core to what makes you tick. Rank them in order of importance. This provides a valuable insight into who you really are and should therefore form the basis of your major decision making (and minor decision making as well if you want true happiness). Refer back to your list of personal core values each time you set new goals. Be amazed at how much more driven you are to achieve goals when they are underpinned by your own personal values. This will help you focus on what matters and to avoid decisions that go against your core values.

For example, I often see clients who are struggling with their budget because they have bought a big family home that is stretching them a little too much. When I dig a little, I find out family is important to them, and so is providing an appropriate roof over their heads. For them, this meant a room for each child and plenty of room to play and live. Unfortunately, they find they have to spend more time at work than they really want to so they can pay for it. Mum needed to rush back to work and missed out on more time at home when the kids were little. Dad is tied to his high-pressure job so the bills can be paid. And they both miss spending time with their kids.

This situation can arise because the true meaning of the 'family' value wasn't clear to them. If they dug a little deeper and discovered that family, for them, meant spending time together as a family, they might not have committed so much to the house. Could they have chosen a slightly cheaper area? Did the kids really need their own bedrooms? Did they need all that space to spread into separate rooms if the goal was to be together?

This is what Stephen Covey meant by the deeper 'yes'. By aligning our spending with our values, we can effortlessly develop and stick to our plan and it will feel like we are achieving what is important.

This is ancient wisdom that seems to have been lost in our modern society. At the core of Taoism is the concept of *wu wei*, or non-doing. This doesn't mean literally doing nothing; it is more concerned with doing what is required but nothing more. The theory of *wu wei* is that if we follow the laws of nature, things get done. If we go against nature, nothing gets done, no matter how hard we try.

If we try to lose weight by cutting out all the things we like, we don't succeed. If we try to balance our budget by working longer so that we earn more money, this leaves us with less time to enjoy life. Saving by cutting out things we love won't last long. But if we align our finances with our personal values, everything is possible; we can effortlessly develop and stick to our plan, and it will feel like we are achieving what is important.

I once worked with a client, Craig, a well-paid actuary with an apparent spending problem. His mother, who was concerned about his spending, urged me to see him. When I first met Craig, he complained to me about not seeming to be able to get ahead despite his good salary. Examining his spending, I noticed he was spending over $1000 every weekend going out clubbing. This included cocktails, club entry and, of course, an Uber and a kebab on the way home. There was also a fair bit of cash spending, which Craig admitted reluctantly was spent on drugs.

The obvious answer was 'Craig, you simply need to go out less', but as we talked the real need emerged: Craig hated his job, and the weekend was his escape. He needed the job to pay for his weekend. He loved the atmosphere of the clubs and the people he hung out with there. The drugs and alcohol were about seeking to fit in.

Craig also happened to be a talented DJ. Together we developed a strategy for Craig to start doing some sessions as DJ, which meant he could hang out at the clubs without feeling the need to spend up on alcohol. Over time, he cut back his day job to three days a week and worked two nights in the clubs. Today he is a full-time DJ. So, by looking at the deeper need, we were able to develop a strategy to fulfil the underlying need and allow him to escape the job he hated.

One bed, one money system

No matter how well you understand yourself, when you share your finances with a partner, things get a little trickier. Now there are two sets of values to consider. What is the best way to manage this?

Conflicts around money are a major contributor to divorce. Although around only 5% of recent divorcees say that financial problems were the major cause of their divorce, most would agree that money conflicts were a significant contributor. Money is such a taboo subject in our society, so this shouldn't come as much of a surprise. So, what is the key to opening up the line of communication and reaching a conflict-free resolution? Two words: values and personality.

Start by sharing your values. Neither set is right or wrong, but it is important that you both understand what is important to each of you. Many values will be common; often that is what attracted you to each other in the first place. But be prepared for differences. Values are deeply entrenched, so don't think your partner can simply change theirs. You need to accommodate both. Also, being aware of differences can help open your eyes to any habits that could be destructive.

Try working through the earlier values exercise together. Understand what your values really mean to each other. Don't make assumptions. On the other hand, don't expect to understand what's really important to your partner overnight. It will reveal itself slowly over time, as you seek to make each decision through calm and frank discussion.

Just as you have a set of unique core values that define you, you also have a set of intrinsic attitudes when it comes to money, influenced by your life experiences, your parents and your childhood. We use a psychometric tool at Life Sherpa that analyses these attitudes and assigns our clients to one of nine personalities. Knowing your money personality can help inform your money plans and allow you to reach a better understanding with your partner. It also provides a useful framework for a blame-free, judgement-free discussion about what matters to you when it comes to money.

The odds of two people agreeing on everything when it comes to money are just about zero. Being aware of differences can help you understand what makes for great money management and open your eyes to your own destructive habits. And when it comes to making most decisions, applying differing points of view can help you to challenge the assumptions you make.

Of all of the personality traits areas, there are three that seem to cause the most money issues in relationships: attitude to spending or saving, attitude to risk, and attitude to giving. These are among the toughest to change – I suggest you don't try to force it. We can all learn strategies to help us adjust and cope. Each of these areas has the potential to generate friction when trying to work out a plan for your combined finances.

To be successful, a plan has to have buy-in from both parties. You need to get to a position where both of you can honestly say, 'Our goals are more important than your goals or my goals'. This is the way to make them achievable. This is not to suggest that you should subordinate your goals to those of your partner. You need to develop shared goals that are aligned.

When a couple sees things differently, there are three possible outcomes. The first is that they eventually agree. After talking it through, the couple may realise that one person is right, or that their disagreement was superficial, or they may find a whole new way of thinking that both of them can agree on. This is great when it happens, but in my experience, it is rare (and not always a positive thing) for a couple to agree on all things.

The second is that they compromise. Each gives a little. In the long term, compromise takes a toll. Money can be so emotional that compromising can be tough. Neither ends up wholly satisfied and it is rarely sustainable.

The third is that they achieve alignment. With this approach, a couple works out a way to meet the needs of both people. They may be doing the same thing for different reasons, but both people's needs are met, and they are in agreement about what to do.

Let me give you some examples of where conflict can arise. The couple in my first example has a classic conflict: Steve likes to save for what he wants, whereas Liz sees no issue with using a credit card, knowing that she will pay it off. He never buys anything until he actually has the cash. She knows she isn't drowning in debt, but it often feels that way to him. These sorts of attitudes are really quite innate, and it is unlikely that either of them will fundamentally change. They may compromise by cutting back on credit card use, but it's likely to constantly bug her, and it will never quite feel comfortable to him.

But what could alignment look like? By getting a better handle on their budget and current position, Liz and Steve gain a clear understanding of what they need to be saving for and how much they need to put away. They can now both breathe more freely and can talk about spending more comfortably because they know what they can afford to buy. Based on this plan, they are aligned on how and when they will use credit and have an overall map for their total spending. Cash or credit is now much less of an issue. They both feel much more in control of what is important to them. They are working as a team toward their goals. Steve generally pays the bills, but Liz agrees to pay the credit card bill because it just bugs Steve to do it.

Jane and Rob have quite different views on risk. Often this is the toughest one to deal with. They have two kids at school, and Jane stays home with the kids while Rob works full time. Jane worries about money and is keen for Rob to have a steady job with a big company. Rob is itching to start up a tech company. Underlying Jane's fear is not really knowing what the future might bring and how she will be able to continue being a stay-at-home mum. Feelings around security are often an important driver in how we feel about our finances.

Again, a plan forms a sustainable basis for alignment. What are their real financial needs over the next few years? With some work on their budget and a solid business plan that Jane understands, Rob and Jane find ways to reduce spending and increase saving. Jane is now more comfortable, and Rob has the financial security to get on with his startup. With this approach, Rob and Jane don't have to choose between security and opportunity but get the chance for both.

The balance between giving to charitable causes and meeting the family's financial needs is the third area that often leads to conflicts. Often this is based on religious views. With a clear plan of what steps they need to take, the needs of the couple can align, balancing the needs of their family with a desire to help others. They start to see what and when they can afford to give. And with a clear sense of what matters to both of them, they can find areas of giving that are motivating to each of them.

In these three cases, exploring their different attitudes helped the couples think more deeply about money and develop a plan that put them in control, allowing them to work as partners to achieve what matters most to each of them.

The first step to all of this is to talk about it. But when it comes to money, talking can often lead to arguments and accusations – so much so that many couples give up on the subject and one person assumes control. This approach is not a win for anybody. Comments like 'If only you spent less on clothes', or 'You always spend more than me', or 'I earn more, therefore it's up to me', are never helpful.

Over the years, I have seen the effects of unresolved conflict in this area, but I have also seen many couples navigate huge differences and lead successful, harmonious lives. I've designed a seven-step process to help you come closer on your money differences:

1. **Accept your differences.** All of us have money habits that can help or hinder us on our road to financial freedom. It is very rare for a couple to have the same attitudes and habits around money. If they did, that could be just as much a problem if those attitudes and habits are destructive. Just as you each have different personalities, which is likely what attracted you to one another in the first place, you also have different money personalities. So, stop trying to change each other; instead, focus on making your differences work for you rather than against you.

2. **Aim to align but be prepared to compromise.** Now that you know how and why you approach money differently, you can find a way forward that works for both of you. Never agree to disagree or reach a compromise that leaves no one is happy.

A sustainable solution requires buy-in from both of you. Work at it until you get there. Whatever you do, keep talking. Watch out for the two most dangerous money phrases: 'Whatever you think, sweetheart', and, 'Don't worry, I've got it under control'. If you don't understand, keep talking until you do. If it's too complicated to explain, don't do it.

3. **Set money goals together.** Shared money goals are essential. Make sure your goals address the needs and wants of both of you, because your shared goals are only sustainable if you both feel that 'our goals are more important than my goals'. Create shared goals for spending, saving and debts.

4. **Schedule regular 'money moments'.** Think about your last money fight. Were you tired or pre-occupied? Maybe you just got home from work, or were watching TV. These are the worst times to talk about money. Schedule a regular time – I call it a 'money moment' – when both of you are relaxed and free of distractions. Have a glass of wine if that's something you enjoy. But never mix a date night with your money moment. Enjoy them separately! Use your money moment to review where you're at financially, identify issues and set some goals. Agree on a set of rules; or you can try my '10 golden rules for talking money with your honey' at www.lifesherpa.com.au/livethelife.

5. **Allow for guilt-free spending.** I usually counsel against keeping secrets in a relationship, but there is one secret all couples should keep from each other. I encourage clients to set up a separate fund in their budgets for personal spending. This is designed to be their own personal secret stash, to be spent as they see fit. No questions, no guilt and no recriminations. When you are tracking your spending, you only need to count the transfer into this account. Where it goes is nobody's business – as long as it is legal! It doesn't have to be big; it's totally up to you. For me,

there is nothing less romantic than a surprise gift that was paid for from the joint account.

6. **Agree on all expenses over a certain threshold.** Forgiveness may seem easier to get than permission, but harmonious couple finances just don't work well that way. Agree on a threshold where both parties must agree on spending above this amount (for things not already in the budget). The limit will vary depending on how tight your budget is. The upshot of this is not to sweat the small stuff. If you can do it within your budget without pushing anything else out, just do it.

7. **Bring in a third party.** A financial coach can really get your finances soaring. A good coach has seen it all when it comes to couples' finances. A good coach is part psychologist, part accountant, but most of all, someone with the perspective of an outsider to help you discuss and mitigate issues.

Setting goals

Once you've identified your core values and are on the same page as your partner, it's time to set goals that help you live a life that is consistent with those values. When you set goals this way, you are better positioned to get the most from the money you have, and to keep to a budget that supports rather than restricts you.

Your goals should embrace your entire life. It is useful to sort them into four categories: personal, health, financial and career. Then look at three time periods: one, five and ten years. This creates twelve categories (four areas times three time periods), so don't get too carried away – limit yourself to one or two goals in each category. But you don't need to set a goal in every category. Keep in mind that some short-term goals may support long-term ones.

Financial goals are usually a consequence of, or a precursor to, other goals. For example, you might set a career goal to be the owner of your own yoga studio in five years. This may require you to pay for some training courses in the short term, and pay for the fit-out and launch of the studio in the five-year period. It will likely create health goals as well, such as fitness and flexibility.

On their own, financial goals may not have much meaning. For example, in 1983, as a 20-year-old final-year student at Trinity College Dublin preparing to emigrate to the UK, I set a goal with a small group of friends of earning £25,000 by the time we turned 25. It was a fairly audacious goal back then. My first job paid £6900, and £25,000 could get you a small flat in certain parts of London. It ticked all the boxes when it came to goals: it was specific, measurable, time-bound and a bit of a stretch. Helped along by a bit of inflation, a good proportion of us achieved it; in my case, it helped that I completed an MBA.

So, why did I wake up on my 25th birthday with a hangover and a deep sense of, 'Is that it?' The missing ingredient was the significance. There was no emotional hook. There was no sense of 'If I achieve this goal, I will feel [insert emotion here] or be able to do [insert life goal here]'. The goal was achieved, but the success was empty. Be guided by your values so you don't get too carried away.

Eleven ways to achieve your goals every time

1. **Break it down.** Break big goals down into a few smaller goals. For example, if your goal is to complete a marathon in a year's time, set a goal you can achieve sooner that will help you get there, such as completing a five-kilometre run in three months' time. This is the secret to the success of programs such as Couch to 5k, now available as an app: C25K breaks down the effort of going from a sedentary life to being able to run five kilometres without stopping into a step-by-step, 12-week plan.

2. **Identify the first step.** You don't need a detailed action plan for each goal – or even each step – but you do need to identify the next action so you can get started and build up some momentum.

3. **Write it down.** An unwritten goal is just a dream. Writing it down creates clarity and helps build commitment. Write your goal in the present tense, as if it has already been achieved. This helps your brain accept that the goal is not just a dream – it can be reality.

4. **Make it specific and measurable.** The only way to be sure you have achieved a goal is with metrics. How will you measure success? How will you know your goal has been reached? A goal to lose weight is meaningless because it lacks a metric. A goal to lose five kilograms by March sets a clear path to achievement.

5. **Use positive language.** A goal should look and feel positive. Articulate what you will do, not what you won't. This helps focus your energy on the outcome, rather than on the actions or behaviours you want to stop. Replace 'I will eat less junk food' with 'I eat fruit in the morning', as if it's already happening.

6. **Give your goal a deadline.** A goal without a deadline is just wishful thinking. A deadline creates a sense of urgency, forcing you to pay attention. Write down the month as well as the year. Don't overthink it; just pick a date.

7. **Stretch yourself.** But don't go crazy. Be realistic: a goal just outside your comfort zone is more compelling than a 'walk in the park'. If you have to stretch yourself, you're more likely to achieve your goal and feel extra special when you do.

8. **Keep your goals visible.** The more often you can see them, the better. Stick your goals on a noticeboard, on the fridge or even on the bathroom mirror – wherever works best for you. Goals that are front of mind are more likely to be achieved. Don't forget to review them regularly.

9. **Tell someone.** You are much more likely to achieve your goals if you commit to them by telling someone. It doesn't matter who you tell: your partner, your BFF or a colleague. Pick someone who will call you out on it if you slack off.

10. **Make your goal compelling.** The most effective goals are emotionally compelling. What personal reason do you have for doing this, or wanting this outcome? How will you feel when you have achieved it? The reason becomes your incentive. For example, a bride-to-be is more likely to succeed at losing weight for her big day than for a random Sunday in June. You are also much more likely to feel great when you have achieved a compelling goal.

11. **Start on a meaningful day.** Research shows that resolutions that commence on emotionally meaningful days, such as New Year's Day, birthdays (especially milestone birthdays), graduations or on your engagement day are much more likely to be achieved.

Summary

· The world has changed since your parents' and grandparents' time. You can't win today's money game playing by yesterday's money rules.

· The rest of your life is built upon the foundations you lay in your 20s and 30s, so build them wisely!

· To achieve peace with your money, you need to truly understand yourself. Your money plan should reflect your core values.

· If you share your finances with a partner, you need to agree upon shared money goals. These shared goals are more important than your goals as individuals.

· Your goals should embrace your entire life and should cover the categories of personal, health, financial and career.

Spend less than you earn

'Budget' is a word that seems synonymous with deprivation and restriction – but it doesn't have to be that way. A budget is really about telling your money what to do, rather than letting it tell you what to do. A well-constructed budget feels liberating, not restrictive. It provides stress relief rather than adding to the things you have to worry about. It frees you from the mental effort of having to think every time you want to spend something.

A good budget gives you the freedom of knowing ahead of time what you can spend and when. It frees you from having to think about how close payday is. And it frees you from having to juggle bills. A well-constructed budget will have balance, and will align with your values and help you reach your goals, all while you live life on your terms. An aligned budget is a powerful tool to help you decide between what you want right now and what you truly want, without relying on willpower. In short, it's about living the life you want with the money you have.

Budgets don't work

Budgets don't work. There, I said it! You might find this a little strange coming from someone like me, when I have dedicated much of my life to helping people just like you get more life from their money. But the truth is that most people struggle to build and stick to a budget for any length of time.

If budgets did work, we'd all be skinny millionaires. We'd all have flat stomachs and bulging wallets. Instead we have flat wallets and... well, you know what I mean.

Of course, I'm not suggesting that you don't need to spend less than you earn or that you don't need a plan for your money. Of course you do. What I am saying is that budgeting as you know it is broken. And I'm about to show you a better way that does work.

Earlier, I demonstrated how the world has changed and the impact this has had on the money game. This means we need to learn a new set of rules to thrive in the new-look world. The number-one reason budgets have such a bad reputation is that they are primarily focused on cutting.

The first question most people start with when setting a budget is, 'What can I do without?' or 'What can I spend less on?' This is the same as starting a diet by asking, 'What shall I cut out?' rather than 'What nutrition do I need?' It's based on deprivation, on just saying NO. It relies heavily on willpower. So, it's no wonder it doesn't work for most people.

For most people, budgeting isn't a rationing problem – it's an allocation and optimisation problem. This distinction may sound like semantics, but it is vital for building a sustainable budget. Let me explain.

You may know that when it comes to eating, the average adult woman needs to consume around 8000 kj a day to stay healthy. But nobody would suggest that a breakfast consisting of a Starbucks Venti whole-milk white chocolate mocha with whipped cream (2591 kj) and four Krispy Kreme Choc Iced Custard Doughnuts (1340 kj each) for a total of 7951 kj and then fasting for the rest of the day would be a healthy diet. It certainly meets the overall kilojoule limit, but means you'd miss out on vital nutrients.

So it is with our money. Although every dollar we spend has the same impact on our bank balance, what it's spent on and when it is spent can have a hugely differing impact on the satisfaction we get and, ultimately, on how we feel about our money and its place in our lives. This means it's not about rationing (simply ensuring we spend less than we earn). The challenge is to allocate our money in a way that optimises our psychological wellbeing. How it's allocated matters as much or more as how much is spent.

Our challenge today is less 'How do I survive until I get some more money?' and more 'What do I need to do with an income that usually far exceeds a mere subsistence?'

The next biggest reason budgets as we know them don't work is because we have been taught to think about what we spend in terms of needs and wants. Needs are to be satisfied first and only then should we spend money on wants. This approach of splitting our spending into needs and wants leads us to start by focusing on cutting the wants. It also leads to us believing that these so-called wants are less valuable.

It doesn't change if we relabel them as 'splurges', 'smiles', 'luxuries' or whatever else. This binary choice between needs and wants leads to feelings of guilt and shame around spending on items categorised as 'wants', and it underplays the opportunities to save on the so-called needs – neither of which is helpful when it comes to managing our money. It's also quite hard work, as I'll show shortly. But this concept is so ingrained that it's tough to accept it is all wrong.

I usually play a game of 'Need or Want' when I run workshops on budgeting for our members at Life Sherpa. I choose a common purchase and ask the group to vote on whether they think it's a need or a want. As an example, let's have a look at underwear. Pretty uncontroversial, you would think. But that's not what the results usually reveal.

When I ask the group whether they think underwear is a need or a want, almost everybody agrees at first that it is a need. We have to wear it every day for modesty, for comfort and for warmth.

So, I ask the same question in a slightly different way. Is a Bonds bra and briefs set at $56.90 a need or want? A few less people are now adamant that underwear is a need. What if we step up to Calvin Klein? At $79.95, is it a need or want? Even fewer now agree that it's a need. A few now think that Calvin Klein underwear is a want but underwear itself is a need. Now what about Victoria's Secret underwear at $140? Much fewer agree that this underwear is a need. Then I raise the stakes a little and ask whether they think La Perla underwear at $275 is a need or want. Hardly anyone ever believes that La Perla underwear is a need. Almost everyone agrees that it's a luxury. And yet, we all agreed at the beginning that underwear is a need.

What's the difference? Price is clearly a difference – at some point along the way from unpriced underwear as a concept to handmade silk, almost the entire group changed their mind. What else might be causing them to change their view? Judging something as a need or want is not black and white, and it's not wise to try to make this decision when you are right there in the shop with the garments in your hand and a 'Sale' sign waving over your head.

Even a simple coffee at home can cause grief in the division of spending into needs and wants. By way of illustration, I want to share with you a post in a Facebook group discussing whether spending $50 a month on coffee grounds to make coffee at home was a need or a want. I've changed the names for privacy and because it doesn't really matter to the point I want to illustrate.

Rebecca posts seeking to settle an argument she's having with her husband about whether his coffee spending is a need or a want. She says that her husband spends $50 a month on coffee grounds. He buys a one-kilogram bag online every month. He is the only one in the house that drinks it. Rebecca thinks it's a want and her husband thinks it's a need. She doesn't elaborate, but perhaps if she drank it as well it might be a need. Or if it wasn't $50 a kilo, or if he didn't drink so much, it might be classified as a need.

This type of post is a recurring theme in many of these groups and this one attracted no fewer than 733 comments, each one strongly arguing one side of this debate or the other. So, let's set aside the fact that if he is going to take a month to get through a one-kilogram bag, he probably shouldn't be buying that much, as it will be pretty stale by month end. Let's just look at the comments, which boil down to a few key points.

The price might matter. Jodie thinks that at $30 a kilo it's a need but at $50 it's definitely a want.

Where you buy it might matter. Some said that if you buy it in Australia then it's a need, but if you buy it when you are overseas it's a want. There was also a fair bit of consensus among the commenters that if you make it at home then it's a need, but if you buy it at a coffee shop it's a want. Why do you think this is? Is this just another way of saying price matters?

Who buys it might matter. Many female posters argued that if the whole household drinks it then it's a need, otherwise it's a want. Perhaps that same logic could be applied to baby food!

Others argued that if Rebecca is drinking something that's a want at the same time as her husband drinks his coffee, his coffee is a want. So, if she drinks a cup of tea then his coffee is a need, but if she has, say, a glass of champagne, his coffee is a want. Or maybe it's both!

Quite a few people argued that the price of a 'normal' coffee (whatever that might be) is a need but the extra cost of this specialty coffee is a want. In other words, you can just agree between you to arbitrarily allocate the amount between needs and wants based on some mythical basic coffee price. By this logic, only $218 of the $275 you spent on La Perla underwear is a want, because you could have bought Bonds for $56.90.

I'm sure that every one of these posters genuinely held these views. I'm not having a go at any one of them. What I am saying is that this sort of angst happens any time you seek to split your spending into needs and wants. The truth is that all spending fulfils some need – the key is to identify the need and then work out the best way to fulfil it.

Agonising over whether an item is a need or want is pointless and mentally exhausting. And that's in large part why it's a flawed method of budgeting.

Balance spending

Based on my years of experience helping people get more from their money, I've discovered that our spending fits into three categories.

The first category is Chore spending. This is the spending that gives you no particular pleasure at the time you spend it. Here, the pain of paying outweighs the pleasure of purchasing. Much of this you notice by its absence rather than its existence. You notice your electricity only when it goes off – perhaps because you forgot to pay the bill. When it is there, you may feel the pleasure of being warm on a cold night, the joy of sharing a meal cooked on your own stove, or the luxury of soaking in a steamy, bubbly bath full of water heated by those invisible electrons. But the act of purchasing provides no pleasure stimulus.

This category includes most of what goes into having somewhere to live, stay warm and be safe, cook and clean, eat, earn a living and meet your debt obligations. It's a surprisingly small list, but makes up a large part of our spending:

- rent/mortgage payments (the minimum you have to pay)
- rates, strata or body corporate fees and maintenance (not improvements)
- utilities (electricity, gas, telephone and internet)
- food and groceries (including lunches and coffees)
- car expenses (loan payments, insurance, registration, fuel, maintenance, parking and tolls)
- memberships or licences required for your work
- childcare (for when you are at work, not babysitters for when you go out)
- insurance (life, income protection, house and contents)
- medical expenses
- child support or spousal maintenance.

Your parents might have called these needs or must-haves, but there are some subtle differences that are important.

Notice that I haven't included clothing. Unless you live in a nudist colony, you need clothes. You need clothes to go to work; you need clothes to stay warm (or cool) at home. But for most of us the purpose of clothing goes well beyond these physiological needs. It's as much about the joy of shopping at chic boutiques, the secret pleasure of lingerie under a prim business suit and the empowerment of rocking just the right outfit at a social function. In these cases, the pleasure of purchasing (and wearing) far exceeds the pain of purchasing at the time.

However, I've included all types of food, even though much of it creates joy at the time and might be perceived as unnecessarily extravagant by some. This is mainly to simplify tracking later. You could take a purist view and say that noodles and beans are Chore expenses, and steak and beer are Live expenses (see the next pages).

Similarly, you could argue that your lunch from the food court and your morning latte at the cafe are Live expenses, as you could take a sandwich and coffee from home and save money.

Don't get too hung up on being absolutely pure. Over time, I have applied a simple rule of thumb that if you eat it at home or take it away, then count it as a Chore expense because its primary function is sustenance; but if you sit down at a cafe, restaurant or pub to eat or drink it, treat it as a Live expense because its primary purpose is socialising or entertainment.

Even though you could choose not to have it, I have included insurance, because without it you are taking risks that you probably won't survive unless you have a very high level of savings. Most people would struggle if they couldn't earn a living due to injury or sickness.

I have also included your car expenses, regardless of the type of car. For some, this is a pure indulgence and may be more appropriate to include as a Live expense. For simplicity and consistency, though, I have included it here, because most people need a car for mobility and to get to work.

Most people spend a similar proportion of their income on utilities and food, so what you spend on Chore expenses is largely dependent on three things: where you live, what you drive and what you owe. In a balanced budget, your Chore expenses should be no more than 50% of your income. This can usually be achieved by having a home worth four to five years' gross (pre-tax) pay, a car worth less than three months' pay and no credit card debt.

The second category is the Live spending. This is the fun stuff, the stuff that makes life worth living. It includes most of the optional spending decisions we make each month. I like to think of it as spending on looking good, feeling good, going out and staying in.

Looking good includes spending on clothing, haircuts, beautician visits and cosmetics. Feeling good includes spending on massages, exercise (gym memberships, sports equipment and personal trainers), club memberships and charity donations. Going out includes most forms of entertainment, such as movies, theatre, concerts, eating out, going to the pub, activities for the kids, holidays, and related expenses such as babysitters. Staying in includes hobbies, books and video and music streaming.

Charitable donations are somewhat controversial, as they are essential to many Life Sherpa members. For simplicity, I include them in Live expenses – it's not a value judgement. If you belong to a church in which tithing is expected, however, it will be more convenient to treat it like a tax and take it off your income, rather than trying to treat it as an expense and force it into one of these categories.

I would include children's school fees in the Live spending category, although many would argue they are essentials. Having paid them for 14 years, I can confirm they certainly feel like a chore when paying them – no joy sparked there! I have done this because in many cases they are part of belonging to a community or church group. Of course, you could avoid them by going to a public school, which makes them somewhat discretionary, regardless of how important you feel they are.

You should aim to have at least 30% of your income allocated to Live expenses. It doesn't matter how you spend it within this category; it's entirely up to you. Your values will guide you towards getting the biggest bang for your buck.

The third category is Grow spending. This is spending on the stuff that makes you feel like you are getting ahead, that relates to achieving your goals – whether they are about paying off your past, doing or buying something that's too big for one year's budget, or simply building a nest egg.

Paying off the past (debt repayment) includes any payments to people you owe money to over and above the minimum payments under Chore expenses. This includes your home loan, credit cards, and what you owe your parents or anyone else. (It doesn't include your HECS payment, which is a tax and comes off before we get to net income.)

Grow spending generally falls into three categories:

1. Future spending, including saving for a new car, TV, washing machine or an overseas holiday. These are items that don't fit into a single year's budget but will be spent on things that will be consumed, wear out or depreciate. This includes future school fees and lifestyle assets such as boats.
2. Medium-term goals, such as the deposit on your first home, cash to start a business or putting something aside to build your emergency stash.
3. Long-term goals, such as providing for retirement.

You should aim to allocate at least 20% to Grow expenses.

Instead of thinking about a budget as cutting things out, like being on a diet, think about it as a spending plan, which is more like a nutritional plan. We need to consume a balanced mix of carbohydrates, proteins and fats within an overall calorie allowance to live a healthy life; if these are the building blocks of a nutritional plan, then the building blocks of a balanced spending plan are Chore spending, Live spending and Grow spending. A healthy balance of spending will fit within your overall income and align with your goals and values.

In the description of these building blocks, I noted a goal for each type of spending: 50% Chore, 30% Live and 20% Grow. That's why it's called the 50/30/20 rule.

Why these percentages? It's all about balance – balancing the stuff you have to spend on with the stuff you really want to spend on without stealing from the future.

Keep your Chore expenses as low as possible. In practice, it is difficult to keep them below 40% for extended periods if you live in a city, drive a car and have a mortgage. Letting it get to 60% starts to impact on your choices and your ability to buy the things and experiences that make life worth living, and limits your ability to get ahead.

Try to keep your Live spending to 30%. This is enough to feel like you are not restricting yourself, but still leaves enough to go towards getting ahead.

The 20% for Grow is about achieving your goals. It's not about saving for the sake of saving or simply saving for retirement – after all, that could be 40 years away (and that's why you have super). Goals could be about reducing debt, saving for the future or simply putting money aside to pay for a big expense that doesn't happen every year (so it doesn't fit in the Live or Chore allocations), such as a big overseas holiday, a new TV or washing machine, or going back to university. They're your goals, and your values will guide you in setting and prioritising them.

I don't claim to have invented the concept of allocating your spending to buckets – that's been around for as long as we've had money and has had a recent resurgence in a number of top-selling books, including *All Your Worth: The Ultimate Lifetime Money Plan* by US senator and consumer advocate Elizabeth Warren, Dave Ramsey's *The Total Money Makeover*, and Australia's own *The Barefoot Investor* by Scott Pape.

What is different is how the buckets are derived. They are not an arbitrary percentage of your income handed down by a money guru who doesn't live your life, nor are they based on complex, value-laden decisions around what constitutes a need or a want and what you should spend your money on. This is a simple, sustainable system, and it works.

It's simple because it doesn't take a heap of spreadsheets or a degree in finance. All you have to do is keep coming back to how your spending makes you feel and your three numbers. It's sustainable because of that balance. It doesn't judge what is good spending or bad spending. It doesn't matter what you choose to spend your 30% on; that's yours to decide. It doesn't force you to give up what you really love. You can achieve what you want and still feel you are getting enough love from your money. It works because it gives you a simple benchmark for your spending. You don't need to look at what everyone else is doing and try to guess the right amount to spend on your home, your car or anything else.

This balance between Chore, Live and Grow spending is so critical that I can usually tell where the real problem lies with a new student's budget by listening to the words they use to describe why they don't feel they are getting the most from their money.

If they use words like, 'I don't feel like I'm getting ahead', or, 'I make good money, how come I've got nothing to show for it?', it's usually a sign that they haven't allocated enough to the Grow category. If they talk about how they just never seem to have enough money, they're usually not allocating enough to Live. Like I said earlier, it's all about balance.

Of course, you can change the allocations. They're your numbers. I've worked with many people over the years, and I've heard every excuse:

But I live in Sydney; housing is so expensive.
I'm a single mum.
I'm single.
I just got married.
I've got a good job and I've got to look the part, so I need to spend more on clothes.
The economy is stuffed right now.
I owe too much on my credit cards.

Even so, I have found that 50/30/20 fits most people over the medium to long term. From time to time, the actual split will vary from the benchmark 50/30/20, but over time it does work.

Keep in mind, it's not intended to be a rigid, inflexible split. It's more a benchmark, so if your spending is way off you can identify it, work out if that really matters to you and develop a plan to get back into balance. One thing is certain: from time to time, your balance will shift. In most cases the shift is a result of a drop in income (temporary) or a blowout in the Chore category.

For example, when you buy your first home, the debt payment is likely to push the Chore portion up a bit, especially if the home is in Sydney or Melbourne. Just keep in mind that anything over 60% eats into the fun stuff, which can reduce your options and lead to financial stress. If you have children and one of you takes time away from work to be with them, your income will fall (even allowing for parental leave) and throw out your percentages. You will need to decide to cut back on your Live or your Grow expenses. You might have set money aside for this in previous Grow spending, or you might choose to slow down on your debt repayments until your family income goes back to normal, or you might need to cut back on spending.

When you have been in your home for a while, and perhaps paid off a good part of your home loan, you will find that your Chore expenses will fall. Your Live expenses might get higher, however, as your kids' school fees bite. As you approach this time, avoid letting other expenses (such as a more expensive car) take over. Try to allocate more to your Grow expenses – this may be a good time to start boosting your retirement savings.

When you're just starting out, you may be earning good money for the first time, and your Chore expenses may be low if you're living at home with your parents or in a share house. You are also likely to be looking forward to rapid pay increases as you gain experience and advance in your career. Avoid letting your Live expenses get out of control: you are at great risk of lifestyle inflation. Keeping to the 30% benchmark will result in more for the Grow category, helping you build up a buffer to travel, or perhaps fund your deposit for your first home or investment property.

In any of these or similar circumstances, ask yourself if the circumstances are permanent or temporary. You should develop a plan to get back to balance, but be wary of relying on future pay rises to get you there. Just remember, you don't have to get there today: it's a goal and a destination. In some ways, the journey is where the value lies.

How does your money stack up?

Now that you've got the gist of this first step to financial freedom, it's time to see where you stand. Don't try to rush into cutting expenses. This is about working out where you are first. Gather your bank and credit card statements and utility bills. Set aside some quiet time. If you have a partner you share your finances with, you both need to be committed to doing this. It can be tempting to let the one who pays the bills go ahead and do this bit on their own, but experience tells me that it works better when both are involved. Go through all your transactions and categorise each one as income or expense. Allocate each expense to one of the three categories: Chore, Live or Grow. Talk about each one. This will help reinforce the allocations and help you think more deeply about what you spend on.

Now work out what you spent and earned in the last year. This is important. Research shows that we are better at setting budgets for a 12-month period than for any other period. It catches the lumpy bills that occur quarterly or annually and makes you think about holidays, Christmas and birthdays.

Start with your income. Be careful to use after-tax numbers: look at the money that actually hit your bank account. Double-check your income by looking at your tax return or payment summary (group certificate). Did you get a tax refund, or did you have to pay more tax?

Now write down everything you owe: note who you owe it to, the required monthly payments, the interest rate and when it will be paid out. Don't forget to include interest-free amounts owing. The required monthly payments go into your Chore category.

Any additional payments go into the Grow category. So, if you are paying more than the required amount on your home loan, you will need to split it out – you'll find the minimum payment on your statement or loan document.

As a double check, add up your credit card balances a year ago and on your latest statements. If the current one is bigger, then you are likely to be spending more than you are earning. Don't panic yet. We'll come back to this later.

Next, move on to your spending. Start with Chore and Live. Come back to Grow after you've set some goals.

You can use any breakdown within the three categories that you wish. It's not necessarily how you are going to track your spending later. What's important is that you capture as well as you can what you actually spent in the past year. You can use a piece of paper or a spreadsheet – it's up to you. There is a handy budget tool on the Life Sherpa website at www.lifesherpa.com.au/budget_planner to make the exercise easier.

Don't obsess about the little details; start with the big expenses and work down. If you don't know, make an educated guess. It's best to overestimate a little.

Think about the items in the following lists. Not all will be relevant to your circumstances, but they serve as a guide.

Chore	Live
Rent or mortgage repayments	Hair, personal care and beauty, clothing and footwear, laundry/dry-cleaning
Strata levies, rates, building insurance, essential repairs and maintenance (not improvements), home and contents insurance	Hobby equipment and clothing, coaching, entry fees
Electricity, gas, water, home phone, internet, mobile phone	Weekends away, vacations
Childcare	Eating out, sporting events, concerts/festivals, theatre, movies
Uniform/work-specific clothing	Non-work-related public transport, car share membership/usage
Licences/memberships	
Public transport	Christmas and birthdays
Car loan payments, registration, third party or comprehensive car insurance, breakdown cover, fuel, tolls, maintenance, parking, driver's licence	School fees and costs (school excursions, textbooks and school supplies)
Medication, medical bills (out-of-pocket portion), dental, glasses/contacts, health insurance	Children (toys and treats, pocket money, activities), discretionary childcare (e.g. babysitters)
Life insurance, total and permanent disability insurance, trauma insurance, income protection, funeral plan	Support for parents or relatives
	Pets (food, vet bills, accessories, insurance, accommodation)
Bank fees and charges (annual fees, ATM fees), minimum payments on credit cards/store cards/interest-free credit	Memberships and subscriptions
	Home and garden improvement, household purchases (appliances, furniture), outsourced household services
Accounting, tax agent fees, financial planning costs	Books/magazines/newspapers, music, video and media streaming/purchase/rental, pay TV
Child support and alimony	Lotteries/gambling

Once you've made a list and allocated amounts against the relevant items, work out how your split works.

Add up your total Chore expenses. Divide this number by your total income, and multiply by 100. This is the percentage of your income allocated to Chore expenses. Do the same for Live expenses. The difference between these two and your income will give you your actual Grow expenses (which may be positive or negative, depending on your spending). How do you stack up against the 50/30/20 benchmark?

If your Chore expenses are less than 40%, you are in a great place. Understand why this is the case. Is it because you have a really cheap place to live (such as rent-free living with your parents)? Maybe you don't own a car because you live in the city. Or maybe your income is growing fast. Make sure that most of the difference between the benchmark (50%) and your actual spend is allocated to Grow. Celebrate your success by allocating some to Live. If your Chore portion is greater than 65% and into the danger zone, you are likely to feel pressured. There is unlikely to be enough for the things that make life worth living. Understand what is pushing you into this zone. Is it temporary? If not, focus on the big four: your home loan (or rent), insurance, utilities and your car. If your Chore expenses are between 40% and 65%, give yourself a gold star. It's still worth having a look at the big four, as you will almost certainly be able to save big here.

If your Live expenses are much under 25%, see if the extra is being swallowed up by your Chore expenses. If not, you may not be rewarding yourself enough. Cut yourself some slack. Enjoy life a little! If your Live expenses are between 25% and 35%, give yourself a gold star. Where is the difference going? There will still be some opportunities to get a bigger bang for your buck. If your Live spending is over 35%, your spending will be impacting on other areas.

Examining your past spending in hindsight is a great way to find out where it's all gone and establish a baseline for your spending habits. But it's only one part of the story, and it's vital to understand the full picture before you try to reorganise the way you spend.

A lot of our spending is regular and varies little month to month – think rent, utilities and subscriptions. Much of it can be automated and little is affected by day-to-day decisions. These items are easy to review in hindsight, and so the exercise of doing so will give you great insight into the elements of this that are adding value to your life.

On the other hand, spending that occurs when we decide in the moment to buy something – think clothing, cocktails and groceries – is difficult to assess in hindsight. This requires greater awareness of the circumstances of the purchase, which can be lost within hours of the purchase. To gain this insight, you need to track this spending as it happens.

There are dozens of apps that you can use to track your spending in general, and many are 'free'. These include Pocketbook, Finder, Frollo, Moneysoft and MoneyBrilliant. All of these apps will link to your bank accounts and provide an aggregated view of your spending and saving. Some banks offer similar services limited to their own accounts. Some are free or offer a free tier with the ability to upgrade to a premium service for a small monthly fee. Remember, if it's free, they are probably making money from your data. At Life Sherpa, we provide a tracking tool as part of our basic subscription.

These apps do one thing well: aggregate your spending across multiple accounts and banks. Some also provide budgeting tools. But what none of them can do is provide you with the awareness of your spending decisions in the moment. That's why I want you to try to track your spending. Sure, use an app for overall spending, but for the day-to-day stuff I want you to record the circumstances, not just the amount and the merchant. Do this for just 30 days and you will develop a powerful sense of why you spend what you spend, and this will help you better plan your future spending.

I don't want you to give up anything. I don't want you to change your habits, just do what you normally do – but be mindful. This is about recording what you spend, where you spent it and, just as importantly, how you felt when you spent it.

When I say all of your day-to-day spending, I do mean all of it: cash, EFTPOS, credit card, debit card, even what you borrowed from your mate and what you spent on others – down to the last cent.

The most effective way to gain this sense of awareness is to record the circumstances as close in time to the event as possible. It doesn't really matter how you do it, but the act of writing it down (even in a note-taking app) has been shown to improve recall.

I want you to record:

- the exact amount, no estimating or rounding
- where you spent it
- how you paid for it – cash, credit or regular payment
- how you felt at the time – were you bored, hungry, or was it habit?
- who you were with or if you were alone.

Then spend a few moments each evening to reflect on your spending. How do you feel? (If you miss a day or two, don't worry too much.)

At first, you may find it difficult or irritating, but the initial excitement of the new challenge will help motivate you. And it will get easier. By the end of the first week, any difficulty will fade as the system becomes a habit and gets easier to keep up. By week two, you are likely to start enjoying your nightly reflection – you'll have the system down pat, and you may be surprised by how many little transactions happen each day. As week three progresses, things should really start to click. You won't even notice the effort of jotting down your notes; it will have become a natural extension of every transaction. You may even start to change some spending habits here and there because you have to write it down. This is a great side effect, but it's not the object of the exercise. By week four, you will have developed a good sense of what, where and why you spend.

Often, awareness is all you need in order to create genuine change, which is why I want you to complete this 30-day 'financial awakening' before moving on to see what spending habits you want to change.

When you've finished the 30 days of tracking, try to draw some overall conclusions. For your day-to-day spending, look for spending triggers. Do you spend because you are bored? Do you always buy a coffee at 11 a.m.? Maybe spending is just something to do at lunchtime? Are there some friends who lead you to spend more than you really want to?

Now compare the total spending shown in the app you have chosen with your original list of where you spend. Is there much difference? Make any necessary changes to your numbers. Has this changed your Chore/Live/Grow split?

Calculate your hourly rate

Most of us exchange hours for dollars. We go to work and earn a salary or wage. In some cases, we are paid at a certain hourly rate, but for many people it is all rolled up in a single annual salary and paid fortnightly or monthly. Then, of course, there are things taken out of our pay before we get it, such as taxes and super, and maybe union fees. There are only so many hours in a year, and an hour spent working is an hour not available to do something else. So, how much is an hour really worth?

When you know this, it becomes easier to understand that what you are about to spend on something has actually taken a number of hours to earn. Understanding the exchange rate between hours worked and cash spent is a powerful tool for aligning your spending with your values.

To work out the true value of an hour, start by figuring out how much you earn. Make a list of all your jobs. Most of us will have just one job, but some will have a number of jobs. Get a piece of paper or open your notes app and list them all across the top of the page.

Under each job, write down how much you actually took home in the last year – that is, *after* tax and other deductions. The easiest way to do this is usually to look at the deposits in your bank statements. For simplicity, I want you to ignore your super – it's your money and it comes from working, but you can't spend it today, so let's just ignore it for now.

Next, work out the costs of earning this money. You've got to get to work, so you will have bus or train fares, or perhaps car costs such as tolls, petrol and parking. You may also have childcare costs. Other costs might include uniforms, training and contributing to colleagues' farewell gifts. List these under the relevant job heading. Add up all the amounts you receive and deduct the total of the costs. This is the net amount you earn from your jobs.

Then it's time to work out how many hours you spend each year to earn that money. Be honest!

List everything you do that you wouldn't do if it weren't for your job. List the number of hours you actually spend at work, including your lunch break. List the time it takes to get to and from work. Include the time it takes you to deal with any childcare drop-off and pick-up. Include the time you spend on business dinners and 'optional' training, and if you travel out of town or overseas, include most of your waking hours for those periods, too. Add up all of these hours.

Divide your net take-home pay, after costs, by this number. This is your actual hourly rate. Does it surprise you? It is also useful to divide this number into 100, to work out how many hours you need to spend on work and work-related stuff to earn $100. Armed with your actual hourly rate and how many hours it takes you to earn $100, you can focus your spending decisions.

I suggest you record these numbers on your smartphone, or on a piece of paper in your wallet, so they are always there when you are spending. Don't be tempted, though, into using these numbers alone as an excuse to outsource things like cleaning or ironing, just because the cleaner charges less per hour than you make – unless you plan to work the extra hour to pay their bill.

Knowing your hourly rate will give you added perspective on your spending.

Getting more out of your money

Getting more out of your money is not about cutting out the stuff you really like. It's about getting rid of the stuff that's getting in the way of what you really want. Remember the title of this book: Live the life *you want* with the money you have. Trim the fat so you can get through to the meat of the goals that really matter to you.

I am a big believer in starting with the stuff that can make the biggest difference with the fewest decisions. Why make 365 little decisions when you can make one that gives you the same outcome?

If you take the advice of most media commentators when it comes to trimming your spending, you would start by cutting out your morning latte. It's true that, as we calculated earlier in the book, if you gave up your morning latte you could (theoretically) save $1387 over the year. To achieve this, however, you must decide not to stop off at your favourite cafe every morning, which means 365 (daily) reminders of what you're giving up. That's also 365 opportunities to fall off the wagon.

On the other hand, you could achieve the same outcome by reducing the interest rate on your $450,000 home loan by just 0.5%.

At the time of writing, variable interest rates on a standard home loan range from 2.19% to 4.32% – a difference of 2.13%. This equates to a difference of $526 in the monthly payment on a typical $450,000 loan, which adds up to $6312 over a full year – that's more than four lattes a day!

The big four

For some quick wins, start by reviewing the big four: your home loan or rent, utilities, insurance and debts.

If you have a home loan, then the mortgage rate you are paying can really make a huge difference, for a small amount of effort. Your home loan is something you should review regularly – a good broker should keep an eye on it for you, especially if you have had your mortgage for four or more years, have a honeymoon or fixed-rate period that has expired or is about to expire, have a property that has risen in value since you took out your loan, are in a better financial position than four or five years ago, or no longer need some features in your existing loan. You will almost certainly be able to achieve some savings. There may be some costs involved, so enlist the help of a professional. See Step 7 for more on buying a home.

If you are in a rental property, your rent is likely to be your largest recurring expense; make sure you are getting value for it. Compare your rent against similar properties in your area. When your landlord seeks to increase your rent, ask what comparable properties they used to determine the rent. Consider whether the property is right for you.

Next, look at your utilities. Gas, electricity, phone and internet bills account for more than 5% of most household budgets. All are very competitive markets and there are plenty of opportunities to save. If you combine your gas and electricity supplier, you can often get significant discounts – sometimes up to 15%. But the cheapest provider of electricity will often not be the cheapest gas provider, so you may not realise the full saving. Be careful of using comparison websites, which may not cover all providers and may receive commissions for signing you up. Don't be pressured into signing up on the spot. Contracts have to include a ten-day cooling off period by law, during which you can cancel, but this can involve a fair bit of hassle.

Here are some things to think about:

· Is the discount on offer only if I actually pay on time? What rate will I pay if I miss the payment date?
· Do they offer flexible payment options (such as monthly payments to even out the seasonal usage fluctuations)?
· Am I locked into my contract?
· Are there extra costs or exit fees?
· Can the price change during my contract period?
· What happens at the end of the contract period?
· Does the plan suit the way I use energy? (For example, have you got solar installed, do you have a smart meter, or can you use off-peak pricing?)
· Are any price changes planned?
· Is the price different if I choose to get paper bills? (Email bills can be easier to overlook, so you might be more likely to pay late – you can avoid this by setting a reminder in your calendar, or setting up an automatic payment.)
· Do I want to pay more to use renewable energy?

You can also make savings by looking at reducing your usage. As with your overall spending, focus on the big wins and be careful with sacrificing stuff you love. Taking shorter showers and installing low-flow showerheads may save money but, for me, nothing beats the luxury of a long, hot shower under a rain head. Know what is important to you.

It may be easier to look at heating and cooling – your clothes dryer and your hot water supply are often your biggest expenses.

Fixing draughts, insulating your home, drying clothes on the line and using fans rather than the air conditioner when possible can yield big savings with little effort. Similarly, appliances left on standby can account for up to 10% of your consumption; switching these off at the power point can yield easy savings. However, I gave up telling my son to turn off the lights when not in use. My own father had a lot more success in this department! Know which battles to fight.

You can also make savings by bundling your internet, phone and mobile, or by abandoning your fixed-line services and relying on mobile. The Australian Communications and Media Authority (ACMA) reports that 60% of Australians over 18 years old have abandoned their fixed-line phones and, perhaps more surprising, 16% rely on their mobile data plan as their sole source of after-hours internet. It seems to me that phone providers deliberately set out to make it more complicated than it really needs to be. There is no unbiased source of comparisons, and the standard comparisons mandated by ACMA don't seem to make things easier. In general, though, I find that capped plans offer the best balance between price and the comfort of a consistent monthly bill. At the time of writing, you can get an unlimited call plan with 30 gigabytes of data for as little as $30 a month if you are happy to forgo the benefits of 5G and have your own handset.

The key to saving seems to be to make sure your plan aligns with your usage (excess call and data charges can be painful) and to take advantages of special offers when they arise.

I cover insurance in more detail in Step 4, but there is great scope to make positive changes here. For most people, insurance will account for 5% or more of their budget. It adds up when you consider there's insurance for yourself (life insurance, income protection, health funds), for your home (home and contents) and for your car (third party, comprehensive). Make sure you have just what you need and get the best deal. Make a list of your policies and ask yourself the following questions:

- Do I need this type of cover?
- Is the cover amount the right amount?
- Can I reduce the cost by accepting a bigger deductible or excess (the part of the claim you pay yourself)?
- Do I need all the features included?

Never simply renew without thinking. Insurance companies don't generally reward loyalty. Every time you get a renewal notice, test the market. Be very wary of internet comparison sites, as mentioned earlier. Many of these deal with a very limited selection of insurers – which may be owned by the site or a related company – and are incentivised to upsell you a policy with more features and to sell you the policy that pays the highest commission.

Selecting a higher deductible or excess can usually generate big savings. For example, a family in New South Wales (NSW) covered by a mid-range hospital cover health fund may expect to pay $59.30 a week with a $250 excess, but with a $500 excess it would cost only $53.40. This is an annual saving of $306.80. How often do you expect to be hospitalised?

Finally, how much do you owe on debts? Money that you owe, other than your home loan and car loan, can have a big impact on your Chore expenses. That's why getting your debts down is critical to living the life you want with the money you have.

If you do have credit card debts, the only thing that really matters when choosing a credit card is the rate. The rest is just noise. At the time of writing, interest rates range from 8.99% to over 20%. In some circumstances, you can even get credit cards at home loan rates. The difference between the highest and lowest standard card on the average $3300 balance could be as much as $500 a year. Remember, though, this affects the cost to you, not the amount you have to pay each month, which is calculated as a percentage of the outstanding balance – usually 2.5% to 3%.

Paying off debts is such an important part of keeping your budget in shape that it gets its own section – see Step 3.

The rest

After you've hit the big four, it's time to look at other regular expenses. Looking back at your spending, you will generally notice stuff you are purchasing every week or every month. This is the next layer of fat to attack.

The way to do this is through what I call the PEARL method. PEARL is a quick and easy way to prioritise your spending and save more. With the PEARL system, you group your expenses into five categories: postpone, eliminate, avoid, reduce and love. Don't let the simplicity fool you – PEARL is a powerful way to prioritise and keep your spending on track. You should be able to complete this exercise in under an hour and get immediate benefits. The best part is that PEARL helps you get ahead without missing out on living the life you want.

Go back to your budget and look for regular expenses. These will include fixed amounts that recur every month, such as your Netflix subscription, music, podcasts, gym membership or Audible account. Also look at amounts that vary from month to month, such as groceries, beauty treatments, haircuts and entertainment. List these regular expenses. Don't worry too much about the exact amounts for each expense; just focus on the items themselves.

Label each item with a 'P', 'E', 'A', 'R' or 'L' based on the system's five categories.

If you think you can postpone an expense, mark it with a 'P'. Items in this category are often larger and so deliver quick wins. 'Postpone' might include replacing your car or redecorating your home. Keeping your car for five years instead of four can generate big savings without driving up the maintenance costs too much.

'Postpone' can also cover smaller items, so keep an eye out for these. Recurring expenses such as haircuts or even dental treatments can all yield savings. If you get your hair cut every four weeks, and postpone it to every five weeks, you will cut that expense by 20%. If thirteen haircuts a year become ten, think how much this can save you. Your teeth won't notice if you postpone your dental check-up from every six months to every eight or nine, but your wallet will.

The key to making this work in practice is to make those appointments ahead of time. When you are paying for your haircut, make the next appointment. Not only does this give you less to worry about, it also helps lock in the savings effortlessly.

Postponing an expense has the bonus of giving you time to think. You may not feel so keen to buy after waiting for a bit.

Next, look for spending that you can eliminate, such as subscriptions to streaming services, newsletters or gym memberships that you never use. Mark these with an 'E'.

It's easy to build up recurring expenses, such as subscriptions that seemed like a great idea at the time. How often have you taken out a free subscription to a streaming service to binge a TV series and then forgotten to end the free subscription once you've watched the series? Keep those that are important and get rid of any that aren't. For those you decide to keep, talk to the provider about getting a better deal. Many companies keep the best deals for new customers, but they can often be convinced to offer these deals to you if they think you'll walk. Even those you choose to keep can yield savings if you downgrade. For example, with that premium pay TV subscription, do you use all those channels? Can you get what you really want on a cheaper package?

Let's talk about avoiding spending. We all have friends who can influence us to overspend. You know, the friend who encourages you to buy clothes that seem like a great idea at the time but that you never end up wearing or returning. Then there are the places we go to and situations we get into that make us overspend. For guys, this often involves alcohol. When a 'couple of beers after work' become four or five, you may feel less inclined to take the bus and instead spend money on an Uber. Then there's the fast food you 'need' on the way home. Suddenly an estimated $20 for a couple of beers has blown out to over $150. Know your tipping point – and when it's the right time to go past it.

Always make sure there is enough room in your budget for the things you truly love. Mark what to avoid with an 'A'.

The 'Reduce' category is a goldmine, and a favourite target for financial advisers and newspaper articles on budgeting. Skip your morning latte and brown-bag your lunch, they say. This is convenient but dangerous advice. I never advise a client to skip their coffee if it's important to them. Such cutting is a slippery slope, because the cuts are unsustainable, leading to blowouts and disappointment.

However, there are still huge opportunities for savings through reducing. Here are some sustainable options to help you reduce:

- Aim for quality over quantity. I halved my coffee spend when my doctor suggested I cut back. I went from four or five cups a day to two, and none after lunch. I made it a game by seeking out the best in town. It turns out really good coffee doesn't cost much more than truly awful coffee!
- Go to the movies on Tuesdays. Save money on cheaper tickets or buy in bulk.
- Plan your day. Planning ahead and managing your time will reduce the need to spend on Ubers.

A big source of savings is your grocery bill. Most people spend 10% or so of their budget on groceries; it doesn't seem to matter how much they earn, this figure tends to remain consistent. It may seem hard to change this. I don't recommend you try to cut back by selecting lower-quality meats, or switching to home-brand products, or trying to cut out luxuries. It can be really tough to achieve savings if you try to do it this way. Certainly, trying to do this while actually at the supermarket is hugely draining. But there are easy savings to be had. The supermarket industry is very competitive these days. Try a different supermarket sometimes – the chains with a smaller range can offer big savings opportunities.

Then, look at what gets wasted. Each year, Australians waste around 7.3 million tonnes of food – 300 kilograms per person, or one in five of every bag of groceries we buy. New South Wales government research shows that the average NSW family throws out over $1000 in food each year. Buying too much, not understanding the difference between best-before and use-by dates, buying stuff without checking what you have in the pantry, cooking too much and not knowing how to use the leftovers all contribute to wastage.

Tips to avoid waste include planning your meals for the week and noting when you won't be home; measuring portions before cooking, so you're not cooking for six when only two of you will be home for dinner; buying only what you can use within the use-by period; and making good use of leftovers.

Last, but not least, consider what you spend on that you love – the things that are the most important to you. This might include your favourite brand of cosmetics, your travel plans, or good food and wine.

Marie Kondo, bestselling author of *The Life-Changing Magic of Tidying Up*, talks about the Japanese concept of *tokimeku*, when she explains that the key to decluttering is to ask if the object sparks joy before choosing to keep or discard it. *Tokimeku* literally translates as 'flutter' or 'palpitation' and is a key tool in getting the most from your money.

In allocating your spending, ask yourself if the expense sparks joy. Always make sure there is enough room in your budget for the things that do, the things that you truly love, by eliminating the clutter, the stuff that doesn't give you joy. Kondo's theory is that 'human beings can only truly cherish a limited number of things at one time', and that by focusing on these few things, you declutter your life and gain clarity and peace. Cut the stuff that doesn't make you feel good and boost the stuff that does. Focus on what to keep by assessing the joy it brings, rather than focusing on what to give up.

Troubleshooting

Sometimes, the PEARL system isn't enough to bring your spending back into balance. So, what then? First, go back to the 50/30/20 benchmark. Is the imbalance temporary or longer term? Is your income likely to change in the near future? Look at which expenses are most out of kilter. If it's your Chore expenses (the most likely culprit), the big impact is going to come from where you live or what you owe.

If you rent, can you find somewhere cheaper? If you own your own home, can you rent it out for a while and rent somewhere cheaper? Do you need to consider downsizing? Don't forget to consider the costs of any such move.

Can you consolidate your debts? Can you focus your Grow allocation on debt repayment? Paying down your debts will bring the Grow allocation back into line.

If it's your Live expenses that need attention, then focus on those that give you the least joy. Go back and revisit the PEARL test.

Life can be unpredictable, and circumstances change, so it's important to update your budget accordingly. Track your spending against your budget to identify whether you're on the right track or whether things need to change. There are telltale signs that your budget needs a health check. Are there trends in your spending? Do you have the same blowouts every month? Do you overspend on clothes?

If your income changes – for example, if you get a pay rise – rethink things before you get too used to the extra money every month. Use it to reduce debt, or put it towards a specific goal. On the other hand, if your income were to go down, maybe because you lost your job, you might need to cut back on spending while you get back on your feet.

Your expenses can change. Has something big happened in your life? Maybe you bought your first home, got married or found out you're going to have a baby? Or maybe you have more cash because you've finally paid off that credit card debt that was sucking up big chunks of your pay? All of these changes are signs that you should stop and think about your spending. Don't miss the opportunity to really make a difference.

Your goals can change. Has something happened in your life that has changed your priorities? Having a baby, losing a parent or experiencing the bloom of a new relationship can all make you reassess what's really important. When your goals change, so should your budget.

Perhaps you've finally reached one of your goals. Have you achieved something you set out to do? Paid off your credit cards? Got that new job? Good on you! This probably means you've got some spare cash you didn't have before. Think about what you really want to do with it.

You could get lucky and win the lottery or benefit from an inheritance. Whenever you get a windfall, it's important to resist the temptation to blow it all at once. Try waiting a while; things won't quite seem so urgent after a few weeks. Then try the rule of thirds: allocate a third to spending now, a third to a medium-term goal (such as paying down debt or a buying a house) and a third to a long-term goal, such as retirement or paying off your mortgage.

Be smart with your banking

Sticking to your budget can be simplified by setting up your banking the right way. You don't need to resort to complex spreadsheets if you get this right. One of the worst banking innovations of the past two decades is the all-in-one account, which combines the features of an old-fashioned cheque account, a savings account and card access. I'm sure the banks thought it was a great idea at the time and would simplify their customers' interaction with them. But in practice, it creates confusion by obscuring what is really happening with your money and making it hard to keep track.

It doesn't have to be that way. Properly structuring your bank accounts can support your budgeting and simplify life.

Start with the core: your hub account. This account receives the direct deposit of your salary and is used to disburse funds where they need to go. It is also the account from which household bills get paid, other than the lumpy bills (see below).

On payday, you distribute funds among the other accounts by automated deposit.

First, put money into your goals accounts – you might like to have one for each savings goal you set. These accounts should be high-interest online accounts, with no fees, and should not be linked to your EFTPOS, ATM or debit card. If your goal is debt elimination, make the payment to the loan or credit card account on payday too, to save on interest. If you have a home loan, try to align the repayment dates with the day you get paid and make this transfer automatically.

Second, put money into your lumpy bills account. This is the account from which you will pay bills that come in less frequently than monthly, such as rates, body corporate, gas, electricity, insurance, car registration and maintenance. Add up your annual expenditure on these items from your budget, divide by 12 (26 if you are paid fortnightly, or 24 if you are paid twice a month) and transfer this amount automatically. You should then pay all these bills from here.

Third, put money into your cash spending account. This is where your day-to-day personal spending comes from. If you have a partner, you will have an account each.

The final account is your emergency stash, which should also be a high-interest online account with no fees and not linked to your EFTPOS, ATM or debit card.

If you are disciplined with credit cards and pay them off in full and on time each month, then you could use your credit card to make all the payments that would otherwise come from your bills and expenses account or your lumpy bills account, and then pay the credit card bill from those accounts when due. You will need to go through your card statement to work out the split. This is particularly effective if you have a home loan and the money can sit in your offset account in the interim. This can help you pay off your home loan sooner by reducing the interest you have to pay.

If you have a home loan, try to set up as many of these accounts as possible (other than your emergency stash) as offset accounts to save on interest. But check first that the extra cost of having the offset facility does not outweigh the savings. Usually offset accounts come with an annual fee or higher-interest-rate loans, so you need to maintain a high average balance to make them worthwhile.

If your bank limits the number of offset accounts you can have (it's usually one per loan or per split), then pick the account with the highest average balance to be the offset.

I like to have all of my regular bills automatically deducted from my credit card, so I don't have to worry whether the money is in the account on the day. If you carry a credit card balance, look to have a separate card for these expenses (which you then pay off from your bills and expenses or lumpy bills account). Otherwise, you will be paying interest on these amounts from the day they are paid to the day you pay your credit card bill.

Keeping track

Making your plan is just the first step. The key to making it work for you is to keep track of what is actually happening. You can be pretty sure that you won't get it right the first time. Each month, as you see where you are actually going, you can tweak the budget. It may take six months before you are absolutely confident you have a working budget that reflects reality and allows you to achieve your goals.

As I mentioned earlier, there are many tools to help you track your budget – there were more than 200 apps for this in the App Store last time I looked. Some of these connect to your internet banking and automatically collate your transactions. Some are free and others attract a fee, but remember, if you aren't paying for the app then it's likely that your data is being sold or used to sell you stuff. Some apps automatically categorise transactions, and others report these against a budget you have input. For beginners, these automated tools need to be used cautiously. The automation can divorce you from the reality of your spending. The point of tracking is to get in touch with your spending. It is much more meaningful if you have to look at every transaction and categorise and report it yourself.

I recommend you start with a manual method, at least for a few months. Initially, it's more about the thought process. This could be a spreadsheet or one of the apps that makes you enter or categorise the transaction manually. It's up to you. Personally, I used a spreadsheet for more than 15 years, and I uploaded my transactions from my internet banking each month. Recently, I've changed to an app, and it saves me an hour or so a month.

Start weekly. Pick a day each week and set aside an hour to look at where you have been spending and compare that to your budget. Look at the trends. Do you consistently overspend or underspend on a particular item? Do you want to change this behaviour, or should you change the budget? You can do these reviews less frequently over time, but never less often than your pay period.

At the end of the year, go back over the whole year and see how you went. Annual budgets are the most accurate, as a year is long enough to pick up most irregular bills. You can use any 12-month period that suits you: calendar year, tax year or even your birthday! I use the tax year because you've got to focus on what you spent to complete the tax return, so you might as well kill two birds with the one stone. It's up to you.

No matter how hard you try, budgets can go off track. Sometimes this can happen very quickly, with a shock. Things such as the loss of a job, accidents or illnesses that prevent you working, addictive behaviour (alcohol, drugs, gambling or compulsive spending) or marital breakdown can all lead to a rapid deterioration of your financial position.

More often, budgets go off track slowly, perhaps over six months or more. Little by little, month by month, you get further and further from the plan you set down. There are five main reasons for this:

1. The number-one cause is setting a budget that is not aligned with your values or based on too much restriction.
2. Both members of a couple weren't aligned – if one believes their goals are more important than the joint goals, they are always going to run into problems.
3. The budget wasn't realistic. A good budget is based on how you live, not on some idealised life you wish you led.
4. The budget was unbalanced, with too large a portion dedicated to fixed Chore costs (housing, debt, car).

5. You weren't tracking where you are actually spending the money and comparing that to the plan.

The key to getting back on track is to identify that you have a problem. Tracking your spending is the only way to do this:

·   Work out exactly where you are. Write down what you owe, what you earn and a timeline for who needs to be paid when.
·   Establish whether your situation is temporary or if it is more serious. Perhaps your income has fallen but will pick up again. Maybe there were some temporary unforeseen expenses.
·   Importantly, don't beat yourself up about the past.
·   Stop making it worse immediately.
·   Trim the fat: revisit the exercises from earlier in this chapter.

Set some short-term goals. Make sure you still have some pleasures. Celebrate even the little wins.

If debt payments are a problem, consider whether debt consolidation or 0% balance transfer could help. But beware of payday lenders: get advice (see Step 3). Talk to the people you owe money to about your situation. You will be surprised how helpful they will be if you come clean and look for a way to fix the problem. The Australian Taxation Office (ATO) and utility suppliers will usually agree to payment plans. Banks and other lenders have schemes to deal with temporary hardship.

The biggest mistake is to adopt the ostrich approach and stick your head in the sand. Believe me, ignoring it will not make it go away. Often people fear they are in so deep there is nothing they can do to get themselves out of the hole. There is always a way; some ways are easier than others. The sooner you act, the sooner it will go away. Take easy steps and you will soon get on top of it.

Generally, you can stop making it worse almost instantly and establish a new normal within 90 days. But sometimes, getting rid of the debt hangover can take years (mostly less than three).

Earn more than you spend

The flip side to spending less is earning more. There is a limit to how much you can cut, but there is (in theory) no limit to how much you can earn. Many advocate that you should therefore ignore budgeting and focus solely on growing your income. This is mostly used to support the argument that everyone should have a side hustle if they are to achieve financial freedom.

'Side hustle' is often a euphemism for 'second job', something that used to be associated with financial instability. If you are looking to get some quick cash to pay off debt or achieve a short-term goal, this could be a great solution. But the version of this promoted by personalities on social media can be toxic – personalities such as Gary Vaynerchuk, who tells his audience, 'Hustle: It's the most important word. Ever," and urges them to "Stop crying… keep hustling".

This promotion of side hustles has led to a huge growth in the number of workers taking on an additional source of income. For some, this could be driving for Uber, delivering food or completing online surveys for market research companies. For others, this could be selling crafts on Etsy, completing tasks on Airtasker or starting a business.

If you are a professional or creative, a side hustle can be a great way to hone your skills, build your network and showcase your talents. If you have a business idea, a side hustle can be a great way to test the likelihood of success before going all-in and giving up your day job. If you have an expensive hobby, a related side hustle can be a great way of earning money doing what you would have done anyway.

But if you are simply trying to bridge the gap between what you spend and what you earn from a full-time job, you are setting yourself up for failure. The notion that self-employment is the only way to true financial freedom is simply wrong. It's not smart to start a business when you are in debt and in search of short-term cash, as the new business will consume time and money.

True, there are some people who build large fortunes from founding successful companies. Equally, there is a growing cohort of people making eye-watering sums leading our major companies as employees. Either way, the odds of achieving this level of wealth are slim.

Creating a business from scratch can be hugely satisfying. Personally, I have achieved financial success and immense satisfaction from creating a number of businesses, and every day I relish the work of helping our members get more life from their money.

However, self-employment is not a sure thing. Most people are not psychologically suited to the uncertainty and the need for self-motivation. One in three new small businesses in Australia fails in the first year of operation, half by the end of the second year and three out of four by the fifth year. Even when they succeed, 50% of small business owners earn less than $1000 a week.

The flaw with seeking to increase your income as an alternative to optimising your spending is that, left unchecked, spending will generally increase again to just exceed your income, and most people spend most of their money most of the time. This makes it impossible to out-earn bad spending habits. Seeking to increase your income in an effort to outstrip your spending is an endless battle that will leave you exhausted.

This is not to say that you shouldn't seek to maximise your income. Of course you should. But you need to do so in accordance with the values you identified in the introduction to this book. For most people, the best way to do this is to invest in yourself, seek to be the best at what you do, and make sure you are paid appropriately.

Summary

· Trying to save money by cutting things from your life is not sustainable. Instead, seek to balance spending using the 50/30/20 rule: allocate 50% of your spending to Chore expenses, 30% to Live expenses and 20% to Grow expenses.

· Avoid seeking to separate needs and wants.

· Analyse your current spending. See how well it matches the 50/30/20 rule and whether you need to make changes.

· Look into whether opportunities exist to save money on your home loan or rent, utilities, insurance and debts. Then, categorise the rest of your spending according to the PEARL method (postpone, eliminate, avoid, reduce and love) to identify further savings opportunities.

· Properly structure your bank accounts to support your budgeting and simplify life.

· Track your budget to identify problems.

· Earn more than you spend. Ensure you are paid what you are worth, maximise your earning potential, and weigh carefully any side-hustle or self-employment opportunities.

Build an emergency stash

Life doesn't always go to plan. Costly surprises have a way of sneaking up on us. These can come from anywhere. An emergency is not always dramatic or extraordinary, but it generally requires you to be able to put your hands on money right away. And yet, almost a quarter of Australians don't have access to $3000 if they were to need it for an emergency.

Your emergency stash should be used for a genuine emergency – something you couldn't have predicted would happen at that time. Overspending your budget on its own is not an emergency. These are examples of genuine money emergencies:

- unexpected medical bills for you or your family
- death or illness of your parents or other family members, requiring a trip at short notice or financial support for those affected
- a major breakdown or accident with your car, important appliances or your home
- fines or legal expenses

- loss of income through unemployment or being injured so you can't work
- relationship or marital breakdown.

These are not money emergencies:

- nothing to wear
- a sale or bargain purchase
- appliance breakdown (such as your TV)
- expenses that are bigger than you planned (such as your power bill).

All genuine emergencies need money now, and you don't want to be forced to rely on taking out a loan or scrounging from friends or family. For some emergencies there is insurance (see Step 4). Income protection insurance can replace your income if you can't work due to illness or injury. Other insurances that might help in emergencies include your health fund, car insurance and home and contents insurance. But it can take a while for an insurance company to pay. For other events, such as unemployment or relationship issues, it is difficult or impossible to obtain insurance.

If you have an emergency stash, you could be more comfortable choosing a policy with a higher excess amount (the bit of the claim you pay yourself) or a longer waiting period (such as 90 days on your income protection policy) to save money.

For an emergency arising from serious illness, your sick leave might cover the first period of absence. In NSW, sick leave is accumulated at the rate of ten days each year. So, if you have worked with your employer for three years and have never been sick, you would have 30 workdays, or six weeks, of paid sick leave. You may also have accrued annual leave, and if you've been there a little longer you might have some long-service leave. You would then rely on your emergency stash to tide you over until your income protection cuts in after 90 days (just over 12 weeks).

Building an emergency stash should be your most important financial goal, even if you have debts. I know that's a big call, but hear me out.

Your finances are fragile if you are forced to borrow money or resort to friends or family when any one of these unexpected events happens. A healthy stash gives your finances a solid foundation and, let's not forget, peace of mind. With a stash, when an emergency expense pops up, you can access the money you need.

If you are forced to hit your credit cards to meet an emergency, you undo all the good work you have done to pay down your debt. Ideally, you want that cash without additional costs (interest, penalties) or losses (cashing out investments that have lost value). If you do have lots of debt or your credit history is poor, you may not even be able to borrow money in such an emergency.

Psychologically, this setback can be difficult and can undermine your plans to eliminate your debt. Having an emergency stash means having money when you need it, quickly. In contrast, debt repayment, buying a home and retirement are longer-term goals, and the saving and investment strategies I suggest for them are usually based on the assumption that you won't need to access the money any time soon, which gives it ample time to grow. You could think of your emergency stash as protection for your other goals.

Only one other goal comes close to building an emergency stash: paying down high-interest debt. So, try to balance those two goals. Building an emergency stash before you pay down your debt may seem counter-intuitive, given that the interest you pay on your debt is likely to be much greater than any interest you'd earn by keeping an emergency fund in a high-interest bank account. But it is important, and it works.

Focus on building your emergency stash ahead of all other goals until you hit $1000. Only then should you shift your focus to getting rid of your debts. When you have erased your debts (other than your mortgage, HECS and car loan), circle back to your emergency stash and get it up to the level that's right for you.

Then you can turn your mind to the other goals you may have.

How much is enough?

As with a lot of things in personal finance, there is no one-size-fits-all answer. It's a balance between having enough when you need it and, at the same time, not tying up too much cash that you could use to meet other goals, such as paying off debt, buying your home or investing.

Three months' expenses is a useful benchmark for the minimum you should have in your emergency stash. This is not three months' pay. Instead, work out how much you actually spend each month and multiply that by three.

This benchmark is a great start and will usually be sufficient for most people. But the right amount will depend on your particular circumstances. You might need more if any of the following apply to you:

- You are self-employed or have a casual job.
- You have children or other dependants.
- You have a lot of debt.
- Your partner doesn't earn an income.
- You have a specialised job, are very senior or are at the top of your pay grade.
- You and your partner both work in the same company or industry.
- You don't have income protection insurance.
- You don't have health insurance.

- You own an older house.
- You have an old car you depend on to get to work.
- Your parents live overseas or are in poor health.
- Your monthly Chore expenses exceed 50% of your pay.

If five or more points on this list apply to you, then having an emergency stash to cover six to nine months' expenses would be more prudent. As your circumstances change, you may find you can reduce your stash; for example, if you put insurance in place, your dependent parents pass away, your kids leave home or you upgrade your car.

The right insurance plan, including income protection, will help reduce the amount you need. Your emergency stash will also reduce the amount of insurance you need.

When you have your stash fully funded, make sure you look after it well so it's there when you need it. You'll need to agree with your partner on what constitutes an emergency and can therefore be paid for by your stash. When you withdraw from the stash, have a plan to replenish it. Apply any insurance proceeds to the stash. You may need to defer other goals to get your stash back on track.

Where to stash your stash

If having a stash of cash to deal with emergencies is critical to having secure finances, then keeping it safe in the right place is just as important.

It needs to be accessible (but not so accessible you are tempted to spend it on other things) and you don't want to be hit with nasty fees or taxes when you withdraw it. You don't want to be dependent on what's happening in the economy or share market to determine how much is in your stash, and you need certainty that you can access it when you need it.

The bulk of your fund should therefore be kept in an online high-interest savings account that is not linked to your ATM or credit card. This account should be with a bank (ideally not the bank where you have your home loan) so you get the benefit of the government guarantee on your savings. Choose a low-fee or no-fee account that pays the highest rate of interest you can find and has no notice period or penalties for early withdrawals.

Do not invest it in anything else that might create uncertainty as to how much you will have when you need it – for example, shares or exchange traded funds, the value of which could fall suddenly if there's a crash in the market.

If you have a home loan, you should not rely on a line of credit or redraw facility, because you may not be able to access it when you really need it, such as if you lose your job. The bank always has discretion as to whether it will approve the drawing. Sure, mostly you will simply log on to internet banking and the cash will just appear. But sometimes it won't, and you won't discover this until it's too late. It may seem like ancient history now, but many people I know lost their jobs in financial services in 2008 during the global financial crisis (GFC) and suddenly found the bank had cancelled their lines of credit or refused a redraw request. Don't risk it.

An offset account is better, but it is still subject to what's known as the banker's 'right of set off'. In plain English, this means that if you don't pay the bank what you owe, they can take your deposit and apply it against what you owe them. This is a good reason to keep your deposit elsewhere.

Don't obsess about the interest you miss out on by keeping your stash safe. Consider it a form of insurance premium.

If your stash is a little larger than three months' expenses, you can tolerate some delays or restrictions on accessing it in total. You must have access to some of it instantly, but you could tolerate a delay on accessing a larger amount. Splitting it so that you keep some in a one- or three-month term deposit might get you a higher rate of return. Keeping some (but not all) in an offset account will reduce the opportunity cost of keeping your stash.

Some emergencies might mean you won't want to – or be able to – rely on your partner being there to withdraw the money, so keep some of your stash in a joint account that needs both signatures and some in your own names. A three-way split usually works well – that is, keep a third in a joint account, a third in your name and a third in your partner's name. This means that if your partner is injured and unable to withdraw funds, you will be able to access some immediately while you sort things out with the bank or solicitor. This is where a power of attorney comes in handy (see Step 6).

Alternatively, you may need to be able to escape an abusive relationship, or your partner might drain your joint accounts and skip town. Believe me, it happens more often than you think, and nobody ever believes it will happen to them.

Look after your stash: you never know when you will need it.

Make your stash a priority

I don't usually recommend a crash diet when it comes to savings, but getting started on your emergency stash is so important, and it can be a great psychological boost to get to that first $1000 quickly. So, if you are starting from scratch, try a sprint to $1000.

Here's how to build your emergency stash fast:

1. **Set up a direct transfer.** Make building your emergency stash just like a monthly bill you have to pay. Arrange to have a set amount transferred from your day-to-day account to a special savings account each payday. You can even get your employer to make a separate payment direct from your pay. In most cases, all you need to do is ask.

2. **Use lump sums.** If you get a bonus at work, win some money or get a tax refund, transfer 90% of it to your savings account, straight away. The remaining 10% is your reward to spend how you like. All genuine emergencies need money now and you don't want to be forced to rely on debt or scrounging from friends or family.

3. **Sell stuff.** Get rid of all that stuff you no longer use that's cluttering up your garage, cupboards or storage cage. Try to sell it on eBay or Gumtree. Have some fun with friends and throw a joint garage sale. If you're not using that stuff, the dollars it's worth are better in your pocket. Not only will you make some coin, but the act of decluttering will feel liberating.

4. **Earn extra income.** Check out some crowdsourcing platforms (such as Airtasker or Freelancer) for odd jobs that you could do for extra cash. This is one of the few times I recommend a second job or side hustle – see 'Earn more than you spend' on page 66.

5. **Use cashback rewards.** Does your credit card have a rewards program that gives you cash back? Apply these payments to build your emergency stash. What about loyalty cards that give you every tenth coffee free? Put aside the money you save each time you redeem your loyalty bonus coffee.

6. **Cut unnecessary costs.** It's amazing what you can cut out if it's only for a short period while you get your emergency stash to the first $1000. Review your subscriptions on your bank statements and credit card bills. Could you do without Netflix for a few months, or your Audible subscription?

Remember, just like a crash diet, you only have to follow these steps for a short period. A budget built on restriction isn't sustainable, as it will most likely lead to blowouts and failure. As a quick sprint to your first $1000, however, it's worth a good go.

Summary

· Building an emergency stash should be your most important goal, even if you have debts. All genuine emergencies need money now, and you don't want to have to take out a loan or rely on friends or family.

· There is no one-size-fits-all answer for how much is enough, but three months' expenses is a useful minimum benchmark.

· The bulk of your emergency stash should be kept in an online high-interest savings account that is not linked to your ATM or credit card. This way, it is easily accessible when you need it, but you won't be tempted to spend it on non-emergencies.

· Start by building your emergency stash fast.

Pay off your debts

Once you have your emergency stash under way, it's time to slay your debts. Here I'm talking about credit cards, loans from your parents, interest-free deals and other debts, not your home loan, HECS or car loan.

It is important to get your debt under control because it limits your flexibility and is the main controllable variable item in your Chore category. The more you need to spend on servicing your debts, the less you have to spend on where you live and what you drive. It's hard to plan for the future when you're distracted by paying for the past.

Debt is not intrinsically evil, so don't beat yourself up about it. Just work out what you owe and to whom and make a plan for getting rid of it. I'll show you how shortly.

Not all debt is the same. I like to categorise debts as red, amber or green.

Red symbolises danger, so red debts (those to focus on first) arise largely from spending more than you earn. They usually take the form of high-interest credit card debts or personal loans. These are the toughest to get rid of, but doing so gives you the greatest benefit. As they are a result of spending more than you earn, you have to reduce your spending (or increase your income) to stop these debts getting bigger before you can allocate cash to reducing the outstanding balance. Worse still, they usually attract the highest interest rates.

Amber symbolises caution, so amber debts are of less concern. These arise from spreading the cost of long-lasting purchases (such as your home or car) over the period for which you will own them. These are usually lower-interest-rate loans and are backed by an asset that corresponds to the debt owing. As long as your car and home fit the Life Sherpa guidelines (your home should cost no more than five to six years' pay, and your car less than three months' pay) and the interest rate is competitive, don't worry about these. Your cash may be more productive elsewhere.

Green symbolises growth. Green debts relate to growing your asset base or earning capacity – think HECS, an investment property loan or loan to buy shares. For as long as the return on the asset funded with the loan exceeds the cost of debt, there is no benefit in paying these down.

And don't worry about your HECS for now. HECS is not really a loan in the true sense of the word and needs to be treated differently. It really irks me that the government constantly refers to it as a loan when, in reality, it is just an income tax surcharge on graduates. I know there is some accounting smoke and mirrors here that improves the Federal budget by treating it as a loan, and that doesn't change how much it costs overall, but thinking about it as a graduate tax can make it feel less painful. In my work, I see a lot of unnecessary angst around HECS 'debt'.

Here are a few reasons why HECS is different:

- Your HECS balance doesn't count as a loan when you go to borrow money. Banks only take into account the impact of the HECS payment on your net income, not the balance on your HECS account.

- The amount you have to pay each year is based on your income (if it is above the threshold), not on the outstanding balance. If you don't earn enough, you don't have to make payments.
- Unlike many other debts, it also survives bankruptcy. When someone is declared bankrupt, all of their assets are taken to pay the debts and the balance is wiped clean. However, certain liabilities survive this process and HECS is one of them. (Child support is another.)
- There is no real interest charged, although your balance is adjusted each year to account for inflation. However, with interest rates at historic lows and inflation on the rise, this distinction may become irrelevant. In 2021, the indexation was 0.6%, down from 2.9% in 2012. Home loan rates were as low as 2.19%.

For these reasons, there are very few circumstances in which paying student contributions up-front to avoid HECS makes financial sense. Similarly, there are very few circumstances in which making additional HECS repayments makes sense. So, take advantage of the cheap money and easy terms available from the government: it doesn't happen often in your financial life!

Now, back to your other debts. Once you've made your list, you might feel a little daunted by the size of the task ahead. Don't let it overwhelm you. There is a quote attributed to Creighton Williams Abrams Jr, a US general in the Vietnam War, which says: 'When eating an elephant, take one bite at a time'. What he means is that when you are doing something difficult, do it slowly and carefully, and follow a plan.

First, you must know why you want to pay off your debts. What will you do with the money instead? How will you feel when your debts are gone? If you are in any doubt, go back and revisit your values, money personality and goals. This will give you the deeper 'why' to keep you focused.

The process of paying off your debts

Now for a practical approach to paying off your debts. I break this down into five steps.

First, compile the list of all your red debts. Make sure you've noted the name of the lender, the amount you owe, the interest rate and the minimum monthly payment. This will give clarity and perspective on your debt situation. Remember, don't beat yourself up about how you got here; just focus on what your future will look like without your debt.

Next, make the minimum payments on all your debts (including the amber and green ones) each month on or before the day they are due – ensuring they are made on time every month will save you paying late fees and penalty interest rates. You should be able to set up direct transfers to make this happen automatically. These should be in the Chore portion of your budget; now is a good time to go back and check.

The third step is to stop making the situation worse. Remove your credit cards from your wallet and put them somewhere you can't reach them easily.

Step four is to look at your budget and work out how much extra you can allocate to repaying your credit card debts. This will be in the Grow portion of your budget. Until you get your debts under control, you should be allocating your entire Grow budget (apart from the first $1000 of your emergency stash) to debt elimination.

The final step, after you have made the minimum payment on all your debts each month, is to use the rest of the budget to pay down one debt. Don't spread it over many debts. When that debt is gone, celebrate the win then move on to the next one. This means that you knock off the debts one by one and get a sense of achievement as the list of your debts gets shorter.

This type of achievement triggers the release of a brain chemical called dopamine. Dopamine is responsible for the warm fuzzy feeling you get when you accomplish something, and it can be highly addictive. That's why to-do lists work so well. It's been proven time and time again that we are better at achieving goals if they are broken down into a series of smaller tasks (remember what I said about the elephant). A quick win is a good win. Use this to your advantage, now you know you can.

The other big plus of this approach is that, as you pay off whole debts, the amount you have to pay in minimum payments drops, so more and more gets allocated to principal reduction each month. That's why you will sometimes hear this concept referred to as the 'debt snowball' or 'debt avalanche'.

To apply this technique, you have to choose which debt to pay first and then the order in which to pay off the other debts. This is where it gets really interesting. Believe it or not, humans have a natural sense of fairness. So, left to our own devices, we want to pay equal amounts off each debt until the debts are all gone. If your goal is to be debt free, this is unlikely to be the best answer.

Which is the better way? An actuary or accountant will tell you that the answer is obvious: just pay off the highest-interest-rate debt first. When you're done with that, move on to the debt with the next highest rate, and so on until they are all gone. This way, the actuary tells you, you'll minimise the amount of interest you pay, so you will be able to pay off your debts more quickly.

This may seem sound in theory, but it doesn't seem to play out so well in practice. That's because human nature requires us to experience a sense of growth and contribution to stick at something. So, this only works for the very disciplined among us who will just keep going until the job is finished. Finishing something that feels thankless is the hard part. So, what should you do instead?

The method that seems to get the best results in practice is to start with the smallest debt. Then attack the rest in order of size until you are finished. This means you get a quick win at first. Then, as you move to the bigger debts, there is more free cash available to attack them, helping to maintain and build momentum.

This is generally my recommendation, however I have two provisos. First, if you have a debt that particularly bothers you (maybe a loan from your parents), it may not carry financial interest, but it could interfere with relationships, so you just need it gone. Second, if there are extremes among your debts – for example, you have a loan that has a very high interest rate compared to the others – then it might make sense to go after this one first before applying the snowball approach to the others. This is rarely the case, though, as most credit cards tend to have equally high rates (between 14% and 20%).

If you are sure you have the discipline and motivation, then try the actuary's approach of paying off the loan with the highest interest rate first. Remember, though, there's more to it than the numbers: you are dealing with the vagaries of the human brain. You can always nab a bit of extra motivation when needed by hitting a really small debt first.

Speeding up the process

There are two additional tricks to help you finish your debt elimination odyssey more quickly. Neither makes the debts go away, but they can lower the cost for a while, allowing you to get on with the task at hand: getting to zero. These tools need to be used sensibly and with great care.

The longer it takes to pay off your debts, the more interest you will have to pay. One way to reduce this impact is to take advantage of the first 'trick': making a low-rate or zero-rate balance transfer. Credit card companies offer these balance transfers as an enticement to get you to take out their credit card and perhaps get you to use more debt. But you can beat them at their own game.

It works like this. You apply for a new credit card that offers a balance transfer offer with a low or zero rate for an introductory period. When the period expires, any remaining balance attracts interest at the so-called revert rate. I have seen some cards even offer a lifetime low balance-transfer rate.

The new credit card issuer pays out the balance on the card you nominate, and you now owe the amount to the new card issuer instead of the old card issuer. You may be able to combine a few card balances into the one new card. There may be a fee of up to 3% of the amount transferred. The debt hasn't gone away, but you have achieved a reduction in the interest rate for a time, giving you the ability to repay it more quickly. You need to be disciplined and not use the new card for anything other than the balance transfer. The new card goes to the bottom of the list for repayments (remembering that you still have to make the minimum payment).

There are usually over 50 balance transfer offers available from different credit card companies at any time. Choosing the offer that is right for you can take a bit of thought. The main features to consider are:

- the balance transfer rate
- how long the introductory offer lasts
- what fees are associated with setting up the transfer
- any application or ongoing card fees
- the revert rate
- the interest rate and interest-free period for other transactions on the card.

The right balance transfer for you will depend on a number of factors, including how much you owe and how much you can afford to pay off each month, how sure you are that you will be able to stick to this plan and how likely you are to make purchases on the new card before you have paid out the balance transfer. You will also need to consider what you will do with your old card and what you intend to do with the new card when the balance transfer offer expires.

This example may help demonstrate the benefits. Sue owes $5000 on her Visa credit card at an interest rate of 19.99% and has a minimum monthly payment of $125. She also owes $6000 on a department store card at a rate of 22% with a minimum monthly payment of $150, giving a total monthly minimum payment of $275. If she pays only $275 a month, it will take her almost six years to pay off her debts. Sue works out that she can afford to make an additional payment of $250 a month, which would allow her to repay her debts in 27 months. By transferring both balances to a credit card with a 24-month 0% balance transfer offer, and keeping her total repayments the same, she can pay off her debts in only 21 months.

Unfortunately, balance transfers don't always end happily. Sometimes you may end up worse off. Look out for these common mistakes:

- **Doing it too often.** Every time you apply for credit, your credit file is updated with a record of the application, the card issuer and the amount you applied for. Do this too often and you will find your access to future credit restricted. This is very important if you are planning on applying for a home loan any time soon. How many is too many? There are no hard and fast rules, but more than three applications in under a year starts to smell a bit. Make only one application at a time and make sure you have a realistic plan to pay off the balance within the introductory period.
- **Ignoring the fees.** Credit cards often have application or annual fees, which can be significant. The big one to watch for with balance transfers is the fee for the transfer itself. This can be up to 3% of the value of the balance transferred. If the balance transfer period is short, this can be significant.

- **Forgetting the end date of the introductory offer.** The period during which the introductory offer applies sometimes runs from the date of the transfer, but more frequently it is from the date your card was issued or, in some cases, the date the card was approved. There can often be quite a gap between these dates. Know which date applies to your transfer and make a note in your diary.
- **Believing that 0% is always the best rate.** It can be easy to just assume that if a low rate is good, a zero rate must be better. But if you are going to take a while to pay off your balance, a low rate (say 4.99%) for the life of the transfer could be more valuable than 0% for six months. As a guide, the larger your balance is, and the smaller your repayments are, the more attractive a lifetime balance-transfer rate might be and the more important the revert rate is. This is where absolute honesty with yourself pays off in spades. Don't try to be too ambitious; make an honest, conservative estimate of how much you can pay, and stick to it.
- **Compounding the problem.** This is where discipline comes in. Don't let the new credit limit on the new card make the problem worse. Cut up or cancel your old card, or stick it in the freezer in a block of ice. Do whatever you must to stop yourself using it.
- **Using the transfer card for purchases.** Don't use your new card for purchases while your balance transfer remains. You won't get an interest-free period on new purchases, and you'll incur interest at the purchase rate, not the balance transfer rate. You will usually need another card (possibly the old one) for day-to-day purchases, or use a debit card.

If you can avoid these common mistakes, a balance transfer can help you get on top of your credit cards, saving on interest and fees and leaving more for you to spend living the life you want.

The second trick to help you get debt free more quickly is to consolidate your debts. Just like a balance transfer, this doesn't make your debts go away, but it might make them more manageable, and it may save interest. If you have several debts, such as credit cards, store cards and other loans, you could benefit from consolidating them into one loan. This means fewer payments, reduced fees and more sleep.

Debt consolidation involves taking out a new loan to pay off all your existing ones. This leads to greater control of your money and only one repayment to manage. It will usually also save you on overall interest fees and charges.

Say you have $18,000 in debts that consist of:

- $3500 on a credit card (19.95% interest, minimum monthly payment $87.50)
- $2500 on a store card (22.5% interest, minimum monthly payment $62.50)
- $12,000 on a personal loan (8.5% interest, monthly payment $275).

You have three monthly payments to make, with different fees and charges and multiple bills and statements to track, and your total monthly minimum payment is $425. If you consolidated all of these loans into one loan, such as your home loan, it could reduce your monthly minimum payment to $68. Some of this difference in the monthly payment is because the scheduled payments are based on a longer repayment period, but most of it is because the rate of interest is lower. This means more of the amount you have allocated to debt elimination will go towards principal reduction, getting you out of debt faster.

Your home is not an ATM. Withdrawing your equity may sound innocuous, but it is still debt that has to be repaid – debt that still gets in the way of your path to financial freedom.

Debt consolidation works best if you are a homeowner and the amount you owe on your mortgage is less than 80% of the value of your home. If you don't own your home or can't increase the limit on your home loan, debt consolidation can still work for you using a personal loan. The interest rates are usually higher, however, so the benefit is lower. With this example, if you consolidated into a personal loan at 12.5% over seven years, your minimum monthly repayment would be $323. Note that you have increased the rate on some of the debt, but the monthly payment drops overall.

A good finance or mortgage broker can help you work out the best answer for you.

Stop yourself going back into debt

Now that you've extricated yourself from the jaws of debt, help yourself to stay debt free so that you can focus on your other, possibly more exciting goals. One way to do this is to understand why you may spend more when you use a credit card.

Credit cards are more than a convenient way to pay for things. They can also help you keep track of what you've spent by providing an electronic trail of your money. I like to do most of my spending electronically using internet banking, BPAY and credit cards so I don't have to keep notes or enter the transactions into my expense tracking system. I'm certainly not alone in this. But there is a large body of research that suggests that if you're trying to save money, you should leave your credit cards at home and stick to using cash.

Researchers have discovered that people tend to spend more money when using credit cards than they would if they were spending cash. They spend less when they look at their expenses in detail rather than in summary. Similarly, people spend more when using gift vouchers or other prepaid tools compared to cash, but spend less when they have had the voucher in their wallet for more than an hour and it's started to seem more like cash. They also spend less when they only have large denomination notes.

According to the research, this difference isn't just accounted for by the liquidity effect – that is, it isn't just because you didn't have to worry about having enough money in your wallet. Behavioural economists and psychologists have identified two main reasons for these spending tendencies.

First, paying with cash aligns the pain of payment with the pleasure of the purchase. Psychologists have identified the concept of coupling, which describes the direct link between how we feel about consuming something and the experience of paying for it. With cash, the pleasure of consumption is felt at the same time as the pain of paying for it. Paying with a credit card or prepaid coupon separates the two activities and reduces the impact of the pain of paying. Think about buying a book on Amazon. The simplicity of clicking a single button is so much easier and more convenient than entering your credit card details every time. If you want to get more enjoyment from what you buy, pay in advance. This helps decouple the pain of paying from the consumption of the experience, leaving you feeling more relaxed. This explains the attractiveness of prepaid holidays.

Second, we focus more on the benefits of items bought on credit instead of the costs. Separating the pain of paying from the pleasure of buying and consuming also seems to lead us to place a greater value on the features or benefits of the item. This leads to us buying more expensive items than if we had paid cash.

These psychological quirks are a pretty powerful argument for using cash more. Unfortunately, this is not always easy or practical. There are some things that are almost impossible to buy without using a credit or debit card: car rentals, hotel rooms and most online purchases, for example.

Credit cards are not all bad

The disciplined among us can use credit cards for good. They can use them for their regular purchases – as long as they pay the full balance every month. Credit cards offer convenience, and possibly points that you can redeem for cash, travel or other purchases, and they allow you to leave unspent income in your offset account for longer, thus reducing the interest you pay on your home loan (if you have one).

The most important thing to know about your credit card is the monthly cycle. This will help you get the most of out of your card and minimise the fees and interest you pay. The four key dates that make up your credit card monthly cycle are the billing period, the statement closing date, the payment due date and the interest-free period.

These are usually detailed on your statement. Grab your statement and have a look. Using my statement as an example, it shows a billing period (or statement period) of 25 June to 24 July and a payment due date of 7 August. This means that all transactions processed between 25 June and 24 July appear on the statement. This can include purchases that were made before 25 June but were processed after it.

As my due date is 7 August, I must pay the balance in full by that date to avoid paying interest. (Even if I do this, any cash advances during the period will attract interest from the date of the advance. As a general rule, avoid using your credit card to draw out cash.) The payment must be made after the statement closing date and before the due date. A refund processed after the closing date but before the due date will not qualify as a payment, even if it wipes out the full balance. If you don't make at least the minimum payment by the due date, you will usually incur a late fee.

If you make a payment by the due date but it is less than the full amount of the closing balance, you will pay interest on purchases on the current statement and on future purchases until you make a full payment. So, in the case of my statement, if I don't pay in full by 7 August, interest will be calculated on all purchases made during the billing period, from the date of each purchase, and added to the opening balance for the billing period commencing 25 August. In addition, all purchases made during the new billing period will attract interest from the date each purchase is processed.

Don't be fooled by the claimed interest-free period. It is largely marketing hype. The claimed interest-free period is usually the maximum possible number of days you could get (usually for a purchase made on the first day of the billing period). In my case, this is 44 days. In practice, depending on when you make the purchase, it can be anywhere from 14 days (the period from the end of the billing period to the due date) to 44 days. For the average transaction, it is more like 29 days. It can help to align your payment due date with your pay cycle. For example, if you get paid on the 15th of every month, then it may help to get your bank to arrange the credit card payment due date to be the next day.

If you have more than one credit card, however, it could help to have the payment due dates staggered so you can maximise your interest-free days. Each time you buy something, just charge it to the card that has the longest to go until the end of the billing period.

If you are planning on using your credit card to buy an expensive item, such as a new TV, and you intend to pay it off over a few months, then make sure you don't charge any of your day-to-day expenses to that card during the billing period in which you make the purchase, or any other billing period, until you have paid the balance in full (including any interest charges).

Choosing a credit card can feel a little overwhelming. There are literally thousands of options, each subtly (or not so subtly) different from the next. Which is right for you? This is another of those personal finance questions where the answer is, 'It depends'. The good news is that with a little personal understanding, you can pick the card that will do the most for you, whether that means minimising fees and interest payments or getting a free flight every year with all those rewards points.

Despite all the variety in cards, the differences boil down to a few key factors:

- annual fees ($0 to $300, or even more on prestige cards; they are sometimes waived if you spend more than a set limit per year)
- interest rates (on purchases, balance transfers and cash advances, generally ranging from 0% to 25%, more on some store cards)
- interest-free periods (0 to 55 days)
- late payment fees ($10 to $50 per occurrence)
- over limit fees ($10 to $50)
- rewards programs (some attract additional fees of up to a few hundred dollars a year)
- other benefits, such as insurance, extended warranties and concierge services.

Strangely, understanding yourself is more important than the intricacies of fee calculations and reward schemes. (What?) The biggest driver of costs when it comes to your credit card is whether you carry a balance from month to month or you religiously pay off the balance in full and on time. So you need to understand your behaviour, really, honestly!

If you ever, even occasionally, pay less than the full balance due, then focus on the interest rate. That includes 'I always pay it off except at Christmas or holidays', or 'only when I bought a new big-screen TV'. If you carry a balance only occasionally, like that new TV, you might want to consider having a low-rate card just for those occasions and a more fully featured card for your day-to-day spending.

So, what kind of credit card user are you?

- **Emergency only.** If you have a card just in case, or for limited use when you shop online or go overseas, and you never carry a balance, this is you. Focus on the annual fee. Everything else is academic. There are a few cards with no annual fees, most issued by credit unions or retailers.
- **Regular repayer.** You use your card regularly, often daily, spend less than $2500 a month on average and always pay the full amount due on time. Look for a low-fee card with a long interest-free period and a basic rewards program (without an additional fee). Check if the annual fee is waived at your expected level of spending. If you shop online with overseas merchants or travel frequently, look at the fees for currency conversion and for use of overseas ATMs. These can really add up.
- **Frequent shopper.** You are similar to a regular repayer but spend more than $2500 a month on your card. The same overall guidelines apply, but look for a rewards program that suits your desires (cash back, frequent flyer or other points).
- **Revolver.** You generally carry a balance from month to month and may be looking at a way to get out of debt. The only thing that really matters is the interest rate. There are usually three rates quoted: one for purchases, one for cash advances and often a lower rate for balance transfers. Look for a low ongoing rate (8.99% to 14.99%) and generally low fees. If you are considering a balance transfer, think about how long it will take you to repay your carry-over balance. If you are confident you can do it within the period of a 0% transfer (available for up to 24 months), then that is a good option. If not, look for a low rate for the life of the transfer, usually available from 4.99% at time of writing.

Summary

- Not all debt is the same. Categorise your debts as red (high concern), amber (less concern) or green (growth).
- Make the minimum payments on all your debts (including the amber and green ones) each month.
- Stop making the situation worse. If you have to, put your credit cards somewhere you can't reach them easily.
- Look at your budget and work out how much extra you can allocate to repaying your debts.
- Pay down your debts one at a time.
- Speed up the process by taking out a low-rate or zero-rate balance transfer and consolidating your debts.
- Stop yourself going back into debt by understanding what kind of credit card user you are.

Prepare for the unexpected

Life is full of surprises. Some we enjoy; others can really rain on our parade. You can't make the risks disappear altogether – and life would be pretty boring if you could – but you do need a plan for dealing with the unexpected. Being prepared for the unexpected is about building a solid foundation for your finances. It's also about eliminating fragility from your finances.

When thinking about risk, it's important to look at both the likelihood of the risk occurring and the impact on your life were it to occur. For example, some risks are highly likely but have a fairly low impact when they do occur – your car service might cost a bit more than you thought, your child might lose their glasses on the bus, or you might get sick and need to buy some medicine. You can be pretty sure these types of events will occur on a somewhat regular basis. The impact is usually annoying but fairly easy to manage. That's why I recommend you build some fat into your budget and keep your Chore expenses to 50% of your income. That fat, and perhaps a little scrimping on your Live expenses for a month or so, will allow you to deal with most of these types of surprises.

Other risks are less likely to occur, but the impact might be a little more serious. These are the expenses that bring your emergency stash into play. You can be pretty sure something in this category will happen every few years or so, and it could put a big dent in your budget – or force you to hit your credit cards or borrow from friends or family – if you aren't prepared. Being prepared for the unexpected is about building a solid foundation for your finances.

There is another category – the low-likelihood, high-impact risks – that needs a different approach. When they occur, these events are so serious that it is not practical to save a big enough buffer to manage them alone. This is where insurance comes in.

Think about your car. If your car isn't worth very much, relative to your income, loss of it as a result of theft or damage may not be a big deal. Sure, it would be annoying, as you would be without your car for a while and have to spend money to replace it. It would be possible to manage this risk using your emergency stash. But what about the damage you might do to someone else's car or property in a crash? What if you injured or killed someone and got sued?

There would be massive costs resulting from this that you simply couldn't afford to deal with alone. This is why the government forces us to have what is known as 'compulsory third party' (CTP) or 'green slip' insurance.

Think about an illness or injury that would stop you working. A few weeks would usually be covered by your sick leave; a few months could be covered by your emergency stash. But what if it were a few years, or even forever?

The human brain is not particularly well suited to assessing rare risks. We find it difficult to distinguish between a risk with a probability of 1 in 100 from a risk with a probability of 1 in 1000, or even one in a million. This is probably why we are happy to buy lottery tickets.

Some risks in this category are surprisingly common. For example:

- One in four of today's 20-year-olds (in the US) can expect to be out of work because of disability for at least 12 months before retirement.
- Annually, almost 40,000 Australians are hospitalised due to road accidents.
- More than 1100 people die on Australian roads every year, most aged between 26 and 64 years.
- More than 1 million Australians have or have had cancer, and 70% of them will live for longer than five years after diagnosis.
- Almost half of Australians (45.5%) experience a mental health disorder at some point in their lives.

Regardless of likelihood, the more serious risks could be catastrophic for most people. And in most cases, the younger you are, the bigger the impact. This might seem a little counter-intuitive, but it is true. The younger you are, the longer you have left to live, in general. So, if you have an accident or illness that prevents you from working, you have a greater number of years to provide for. Similarly, if you were to die, your partner would need to survive for much longer without you.

While some risks are less likely to occur to younger people – you are less likely to get ill or die, for instance – other risks, such as accidents, peak in the early adult years. If you have no dependants or debts, you probably don't have to worry too much about the risk of dying, as it will have little financial impact on you. (Dying is cheap; staying alive costs money!) But you do need to be concerned about the impact on your life of an accident or illness that could prevent you from working.

The secret is to buy just enough insurance. Today!

Insurance is boring but important

Insurance may be one of the dullest words ever. Research from one of America's big insurers found that 6% of the 20- to 30-year-olds surveyed would rather eat an insect than think about insurance. If you've ever spent time with an actuary, you understand. But even though it may not feel as exciting as saving for your next holiday, insurance is an important part of your plan for financial freedom. A few minutes spent considering this now can make a massive difference to your life.

Insurance is simply the pooling of risks among a group of people. Everyone pays a small proportion of the cost of the event occurring into a pool from which those unlucky enough to suffer the impact get paid. Therefore, everyone pays their statistically likely cost (probability multiplied by impact) plus a bit extra to cover the cost of administering the pool and a profit for the insurance company for taking the risk should they get their sums wrong. This extra cost is why insurance makes more sense for risks where the impact is very significant.

In practice, this means you make a monthly or yearly payment (called a premium), and when an event like death, injury or illness strikes, the insurer pays you a single payment (lump sum) or ongoing monthly payments. Lump-sum benefits are usually tax-free. Monthly benefits that replace lost income are generally taxable.

In one way or another, most of us rely on exchanging hours of our time for dollars to live on. Your ability to do that is your biggest asset. If you can't work for a little bit there is always sick leave or your emergency stash, but for any period beyond a few months, few people can survive without income replacement.

It's important that you don't let fear drive your decisions. Know what you need and why. Separate the emotional from the financial. Discussions around who is worth more in a relationship can be confronting but are essential to getting the call right.

A comprehensive protection package will consist of four types of insurance. These four products – income protection insurance, total and permanent disability (TPD) insurance, trauma insurance and life insurance – are often bought as a package, which can be cheaper than buying them separately (although not everyone needs all of them). Everyone who depends on their income to pay their bills or achieve their goals needs income protection insurance and almost certainly TPD insurance. If anyone else depends on your income, you need life insurance. You should also consider trauma or critical illness cover. The cost of each type of insurance varies widely depending on factors such as occupation, age, gender and the amount of cover needed. In addition to these four types of insurance, you should consider whether you need health insurance – but this fits into a different category, and I'll cover it later.

Income protection is designed to replace your income if you are unable to work due to accident or illness (not redundancy or unemployment). It pays a monthly benefit for as long as you are unable to work. This is the most important cover and the one you are most likely to claim on. Generally, you can buy cover that will replace up to 70% of your income, but if you spend a lot less than you earn, you may prefer to look at what you spend as your guide. A lower replacement rate might mean you have to delay pursuing any of your goals that relate to the unspent portion of your income.

You can generally choose the amount of time between when you are unable to work and when the policy starts to pay you. The longer the period you choose, the cheaper the premium. If you combine your sick leave, annual leave, long-service leave and emergency stash, you should be able to get by for 90 days or so before you need the insurance payout. This can mean significant savings on premiums. For $10 a week, a 30-year-old male professional non-smoker could get $5000 per month cover.

For more serious events, TPD insurance pays you a lump sum if you suffer an illness or injury that leaves you unable to work and unlikely to ever work again. There are two types of policies available: 'own occupation' or 'any occupation'. 'Own occupation' provides cover when it is unlikely that you will work again in your own occupation as a result of an illness or injury. 'Any occupation', the cheaper policy, provides cover when it is unlikely that you will be able to work again in any occupation. To illustrate, a surgeon who suffers a hand injury in a car accident could receive an 'own occupation' payout if they were unlikely to work again as a surgeon, but they might not be eligible under an 'any occupation' policy, because they might still be able to practice as a GP, based on their education, training and experience. For $3 a week a 30-year-old male professional non-smoker could get $100,000 cover.

Most super funds offer death cover and usually TPD to their members, usually with an ability to 'opt out'. This means they provide it unless you elect not to pay for it – check with your fund. In fact, the default fund (the one your contributions are paid into if you don't choose a super fund) is required by law to provide at least a minimum level of insurance. Your super can often be a very cost-effective way to buy insurance, and for some people it may be the only choice. However, it's also usually an inferior form of cover and is unlikely to provide anywhere near the level of financial support your family needs. I'll show you later (page 120) how you can still use your super money to pay for it but not be tied to the cover your particular fund offers. This can be great for making the insurance you need affordable when your budget is tight.

Trauma insurance, or critical illness cover, provides a lump-sum payment when you are diagnosed with one or more nominated medical conditions. These range from diseases such as hepatitis C or HIV to accidents that result in a loss of one or more limbs, sight or hearing, and emergencies such as heart attack or cancer. Cover varies significantly between insurers. It is designed to provide financial help while you take time out to recover or your partner takes time out to support you. This is in addition to your health fund claim, sick leave or income protection insurance to replace your income. Most people need some degree of trauma cover. For around $6 a week, a 30-year-old male professional non-smoker could get $100,000 cover.

Life insurance (sometimes called 'life assurance') would probably be easier to understand if we called it 'death insurance', since it covers you for death or terminal illness. Life insurance pays out a lump sum when you die or are diagnosed with a terminal illness (expected to lead to death within 12 months, or in some cases 24 months). This type of cover is easy to comprehend, it's relatively cheap and most policies are similar. For example, a 30-year-old male professional non-smoker could get $100,000 of cover for around $5 a week. Benefits are tax-free and, correspondingly, the premiums paid are not tax deductible to individuals.

It's mostly not about you; it's about those left behind if you die. Life insurance offers financial protection for your family at a time when they really can't think about money. It can't replace you, but it can make sure your family is looked after, giving them options and the freedom to make the right lifestyle decisions. You or your dependants could use the payout to:

· do the things you always wanted to do before you die
· provide for palliative (end-of-life) care
· stay in the family home by paying out the amount owing on your home loan
· maintain their standard of living by providing an amount that can be invested or drawn down over a period of time to replace your income

- cover additional costs incurred by single-parent families, such as childcare
- meet funeral or other immediate costs
- cover planned future expenses, such as children's education.

If you are single, have no debts and nobody depends on you for financial support, then you likely won't need life insurance. But you might need cover if you run a business with a partner, have a loan with someone or someone has guaranteed a loan for you, want to cover your funeral expenses, or have someone who depends on you or might need to depend on you in the future, such as parents or siblings.

For all these types of insurance, there are advantages to starting young. The older you are, the harder it is to take out cover, so getting in early helps you get the right cover at the right price. Depending on the cover you choose, you may be able to take advantage of more competitive premiums and lock in a lower rate for life. As your life situation evolves, so can your cover. This is why insurance is generally not a set-and-forget proposition. Your adviser should review it with you annually – that's why the insurance company pays them commission for the life of your policy. You should also review your cover when your circumstances change, especially when you are preparing for life events such as getting married, having a baby, buying a home or changing jobs or careers.

Paying your premiums

Premiums can usually be paid monthly, although this usually costs a bit more than paying annually. Spreading the payment across the year helps with budgeting and is often worth the extra cost. Income protection premiums are usually tax deductible when you pay them, and the payout is taxable when you receive it. Life, TPD and trauma insurance premiums are not generally tax deductible, and the payout is generally tax free.

Lock in a low rate while you are young and healthy. The cost of life, TPD, trauma and income protection insurance rises as you get older, but it is possible to lock in a fixed rate for life so it will only change when the general rate changes. This is called a 'level premium' and can be great if you are young or starting out. A good adviser can help you work out if this is a good option for you.

You can also take some pressure off your budget by using your super to pay your premiums. You are not limited to just the policies offered by your super fund; you can choose the policy that's right for you from most of the insurers in Australia. Insurance premiums for life, TPD and income protection paid through your super fund are tax deductible to your fund. This means they will cost less. Also, because they're not coming out of your day-to-day budget, it's easier to pay annually, saving you the extra cost of choosing monthly payments.

Here's what the numbers look like, based on a typical premium for $500,000 of life and TPD cover for a 30-year-old professional non-smoker earning between $45,001 and $120,000 (where the marginal tax rate is 34.5%):

Table 1: Comparing insurance premium payment methods

Insurance payment method	After-tax cost: monthly*	After-tax cost: annually
Insurance paid outside super	$358	$338
Insurance paid using super and salary sacrifice	$234	$221
Total saving	$124	$117

*This column shows the annual figures if paid monthly, assuming a typical additional charge of 6%.

You can't pay for your trauma insurance using your super, nor can you include some features of TPD (own occupation) or income protection (premium features). Most insurance companies now offer hybrid packages, which link the stuff you can have in super with a top-up policy outside super for the rest. This is where a good adviser really helps.

Of course, using your super to pay your insurance reduces the amount of your super available to fund your retirement. You can replace this by salary-sacrificing some of your wage to top up your super. This means that your employer pays some of the money they were going to pay you as salary to your super fund instead. Here's what the numbers look like, based on the same typical premium as described on the previous page:

Table 2: Topping up your super through salary-sacrificing

	After-tax cost: monthly*	After-tax cost: annually
Payment into super fund through salary sacrifice	$358	$338
Less contributions tax (15%)	-$54	-$51
Premium paid	-$358	-$338
Tax rebate	$54	$51
Effect on retirement savings	$0	$0

*This column shows the annual figures if paid monthly, assuming a typical additional charge of 6%.

Health insurance

In Australia, most of our health care is provided for free through an extensive government scheme, Medicare. There are a number of services that are not generally covered by Medicare: dental, glasses, ambulance and most ancillary health services, such as chiropractic. There can also be extensive waiting periods for non-emergency treatment.

However, medical treatment can be ruinously expensive, making illness one of the three major causes of defaults on loans, along with unemployment and marital breakdown. The government has a policy that encourages people (who can afford it) to take out health insurance.

Health insurance allows you to choose the doctor who treats you, avoid waiting lists and have a private room in hospital. It can also save you tax. You can also add on ancillary cover, which helps meet the costs of services such as optical, dental, chiropractic and other medical services provided outside a hospital.

Medicare generally doesn't cover medical expenses overseas, although there are reciprocal arrangements with some countries. Overseas medical treatment can be expensive, particularly in the US and Canada. Travel insurance is designed to cover this. It's a good idea to take out travel insurance whenever you go overseas, for business or holidays.

Here are some key reasons to have health insurance:

- You may pay more tax without it. If you don't have hospital cover and you earn over the threshold ($90,000 if you are single and $180,000 for families), your Medicare levy (expense) is higher. In most cases, this additional levy is more than the cost of a minimal qualifying policy, so it makes good sense to take out a policy.
- Your health fund premiums go up if you wait. If you are over 30, the premium increases by 2% each year that you delay taking out your health insurance (from 1 July following your 31st birthday). So, if you were born in June 1991 and wait until 2 July 2022

before you take out health cover, you will pay 2% extra on your premiums for up to 10 years of continuous cover. At today's rates ($53 per week for medium hospital-only cover), this amounts to $56 per year. If you wait until after you turn 40, the surcharge is 20% (an extra $552 per year), and it rises to a maximum of 70% if you don't take it out before age 65.

- The subsidy scheme means the government will pay up to 32.812% of your premium, depending on your age and income. For those under 65, the rebate is as follows (and couples get double these limits):
  - 24.608% for singles earning up to $90,000
  - 16.405% for singles earning more than $90,000 but less than $105,000
  - 8.202% for singles earning more than $105,000 but less than $140,000.

Types of health insurance

There are three types of health insurance policies available in Australia: ambulance cover, hospital cover and extras cover. Depending on what cover you choose, the health fund will pay some of the cost of medical services not already covered by Medicare. The part of the bill not covered by your fund is called the 'gap' and must be paid by you. A number of funds have arrangements with certain doctors and hospitals so that there is no gap.

With ambulance cover, generally the person who receives the ambulance treatment is the one required to pay for the service, not the person who calls the ambulance. The fee varies from state to state and depends on the nature of the call-out and how far you travel. In NSW, this starts from $407 and can go up to $6668 (at $3.62 per kilometre). In Queensland and Tasmania, the state government provides it for free to residents.

Concession card holders (Health Care Card, Pensioner Concession Card, Veteran Card and Commonwealth Seniors Health Card) generally get ambulance cover for free. For everyone else, it's cheap: as little as $50 per year for a single person under 65 in NSW who earns less than $90,000. Hospital cover includes ambulance services in states where the government doesn't provide it for free. Ambulance cover doesn't include costs that are covered by insurance, such as motor accidents or work-related incidents. (Work-related injuries are generally covered by WorkCover.) Some policies also don't cover the call-out fee if an ambulance is called and you are not taken to hospital.

Hospital cover is the one you need if you want to avoid the Medicare Levy Surcharge (MLS). The key benefit of hospital cover is that it covers the cost of being a private patient in a public or private hospital. This means you can choose your doctor (as long as they have rights to practise in the relevant hospital) and you may even avoid the waiting list for non-emergency treatment. If you go with a private hospital, you can choose which one you want. Private hospitals usually have private rooms and better amenities, which can make your hospital stay less stressful. Even if you have private hospital cover, you can choose to attend as a public patient.

The Medical Benefits Schedule (MBS) is a list of treatments and services for which a Medicare benefit is payable and the amount of that benefit (known as the MBS fee). It stretches to some 887 pages! When you are a private patient in either a public or private hospital, the provider will charge you a fee, which is likely to be more than the MBS fee. Medicare will pay 75% of the MBS fee for the services you receive. Your health fund then pays you the remaining 25%. As a result, there will likely be a gap between the amount the provider charges you and the total of the Medicare benefit and the benefit from your fund; you will need to pay this out of your own pocket. Many funds have no-gap arrangements for some services. This is an important feature when comparing funds.

When comparing policies, look at what services are covered. Gold policies will cover the most services. Silver, bronze or basic policies will cover progressively fewer. Cheaper policies generally don't cover obstetrics, assisted reproduction (IVF), heart problems, kidney dialysis, mental illnesses or hip and knee replacements. Also, you can reduce your premium by choosing a higher excess (the amount of the claim you have to pay yourself). This is limited to $750 per person for policies that exempt you from paying the MLS.

Then there is extras (or ancillary) cover, which is the one most people think about when it comes to health cover. It covers optical, dental, physio and chiropractic services. Many policies also provide benefits for massage, gym membership and other healthy activities. Extras cover is possibly the most difficult to compare, because it consists of a number of independent limits on what is covered. Cover for a 30-year-old single person in NSW ranges from $5.85 to $40 per week. If you wear glasses, visit the dentist and use the fitness or ancillary benefits, you will usually recover the cost of your premium.

How to choose a fund

Working out the best fund and policy for your needs and circumstances isn't simple, and a working knowledge of medical terminology will help. It is almost impossible to do it properly without professional help.

Half our population has health cover, and more than one in five policies are bought online through online comparison sites. But most comparison sites do not cover all of the providers in the market. In fact, most of them leave out about half the funds that make up the market, and some focus on their own products.

Think about what cover you really need. If you have three kids, it's probably unnecessary to pay extra for the obstetrics or IVF cover included in most top-tier products. On the other hand, most policies aimed at younger people exclude knee reconstructions and hip replacements; if you play sport, you might want to include that type of cover.

Consider a higher excess. If you choose a $500 excess instead of $250, this could save you nearly $200 a year, so if you don't think you'll claim every year, you are better off with a higher excess. Remember, the excess only applies to the hospital cover.

Consider the motivation behind the product being sold. When you buy directly from the provider, the interests they support are their own. They want you to buy their product, and usually the most expensive type they can sell you. For example, did you know that comparison sites get a commission of up to $800 when you take out a policy? Not all providers pay the same commission; others don't pay any commissions. For this reason, it really helps to talk to a financial adviser or broker licensed to provide personal advice and who, by law, acts in your best interests. A good broker can help source the best fit for your needs and ensure a good deal. For some things, it really does help to talk to an expert.

Summary

- Being prepared for the unexpected means eliminating fragility from your finances.
- Mitigate risk by buying just enough insurance, today!
- Lock in a low rate while you are young and healthy. You can also use your super to pay your premiums.
- Choose a health insurance fund by looking at the inclusions and assessing what you really need. Also, consider a higher excess.

Get the super basics right

One of the greatest money challenges we face in our lives is how to make 40 years of income last for as much as 70 years of adult life. We enter adulthood with an abundance of human capital (mostly in the form of our ability to earn an income) and very little financial capital. Over our earning lives, we need to convert a sufficient amount of that human capital into financial capital to support our lifestyle for the period when we are unable or unwilling to work. How much financial capital we need depends on how early we intend to stop working and how much we spend. This conversion can take many forms – examples include buying (and paying off) our home, investing specifically for retirement (including through super), paying off debts and building up assets outside super.

Retirement might feel a long way off right now, which makes it difficult for you to give it the attention it deserves, especially when you've got a life to live and bills to pay. For most people, it may be best to focus on paying down debt, buying a home and investing outside super, until you are a little older and more financially stable. Then you can look at adding more to your super fund. Whatever your plans, you can improve your retirement outcome with a few simple steps and without impacting your lifestyle today.

Luckily, your employer is required to put away 10% of your pay into your super on your behalf – so if you earn $50,000 a year, you will receive $5000 in contributions to your super. It is your money; you just don't get to spend it yet! Properly nurtured, it will go a long way to providing a reasonable retirement income, as a major component of an overall plan. So, how can you get the most out of your super?

Simple steps to a better retirement

Here are three things you can do today that will dramatically improve your retirement lifestyle, without affecting how you spend your money right now.

First, find any lost super. If you have changed jobs, moved house or changed your name, you could be one of the millions of Australians who has money sitting in a lost super account. In fact, there is over $13.8 billion in super money sitting in over six million lost and unclaimed accounts held by the ATO. Some of this could be yours, and if it is, it's costing you money in fees and lost earnings. You can find your lost super with time and patience. Start by logging in to your myGov account.

Next, round up your entire super into one fund. If you are (or were) like most young Australians, chances are you have had a few casual or part-time jobs over the years. And if you did, it's likely that you have more than one super fund. In fact, three out of ten Australians with super have more than one super account.

The more funds you have, the more fees you pay. Most funds have a fixed administration fee, regardless of how big or small your balance is. Multiple accounts usually mean unnecessary fees eroding your retirement savings.

Consolidating your super means transferring it to one fund, which can save heaps on fees. But it isn't always the right answer – you might lose insurance cover you can't replace and you may end up paying more tax on some benefits. Do not do this without professional assistance.

Finally, choose the right fund and investment option. Choosing the fund that is right for you can be overwhelming, but it can make a huge difference to how well you will live in retirement. Two-thirds of the money you will receive from your super in retirement will come from the earnings on your savings. So, how do you decide which fund will best suit you and your situation? We'll look at eight aspects to consider over the rest of this section.

Start with asset allocation

The biggest single driver of both risk and return is asset allocation, so get this right first before you worry about anything else.

Asset allocation is the type and mix of assets in your super fund. It's the mix between shares, bonds, cash and commodities. It's also the mix within those broad categories – that is, how much of your allocation to shares is devoted to Australian or overseas shares, how much is allocated to large companies or small companies, and how much is allocated to growth companies or value companies.

Some asset types, such as cash and bonds, tend to produce low but steady returns with a low risk of losing money. These are called 'defensive assets'. Others, such as shares, deliver higher returns but with more variability and a greater chance of losing value. We call these 'growth assets' because they are capable of providing returns above inflation over time.

Generally, if you target a higher return, you need to accept a higher level of risk. But make sure that each unit of additional risk you take is rewarded by a corresponding increment in expected return.

For long-term investments like super, mixing defensive and growth assets in the right proportion can deliver higher long-term returns with less variability and risk. Too little growth and inflation will erode the buying power of your savings, while too much invested in growth assets can create volatility, potentially leading to panic reactions. For most people, controlling such emotional reactions is the key to achieving their goals.

Action step: Determine the right asset allocation for your needs. Assess your goals, circumstances, age, plans for retirement, risk tolerance and capacity to recover from a material loss, as well as your money personality.

Check that you are getting the asset allocation you select

As important as it is to work out the right asset allocation for your needs, it is even more important to ensure that the fund you choose will actually give it to you in practice over the long term.

Many of the leading funds' flagship products have a wide discretion in their choice of asset allocation. None of them discloses how they choose where to be in the allowable range. A little discretion is necessary, so that you don't incur excessive trading costs by rebalancing too frequently. But most of these ranges are so wide that the nature of the fund could potentially be completely changed. That balanced fund you chose could end up being a conservative fund or a high-growth fund and you'll only find out afterwards.

Table 3 shows the target asset allocation for the most popular choices, derived from the product disclosure statements for each fund and Australian Prudential Regulation Authority (APRA) publications.

Action step: Look carefully at both the target asset allocation and at the allowable ranges. This is your first filter to narrow down your short list of funds.

Table 3: Target asset allocation across popular super funds

Fund	Target allocation to growth assets	Actual allocation to growth assets*	Range of possible allocation to growth assets
AustralianSuper (Balanced)	78%	75%	30–100%
Aware Super (My Super Lifecycle)	88%	69%	55–75%
UniSuper (Accumulation 1)	68%	68%	50–90%
Rest Super (Core Strategy)	72%	69%	60–75%
HESTA (Balanced Growth)	74%	75%	45–95%
Cbus (Growth)	74%	71%	59–99%
Hostplus (Balanced)	76%	79%	60–76%
Hostplus (Indexed Balanced)	75%	Not reported	50–90%

*AustralianSuper data is from 30 June 2021; Aware Super data is from 31 December 2021; all other data is from 30 June 2020.

Seek transparency

Australia's super funds have long had a culture of secrecy about their investments and how they choose them, leaving fund members in the dark over how their retirement savings are being invested. As a result, it is impossible in many cases for members (or their professional advisers) to assess how the returns were achieved and whether they are appropriate for the risk taken. It means that Australians have been given choice over where their retirement savings are invested, but the information to make that decision meaningful is being withheld.

Morningstar reports that Australia ranks at the bottom of 26 global markets for investment portfolio disclosure. This result is so bad that Australia is in the bottom category all on its own. Rest Super recently spent an undisclosed amount of their members' money defending their refusal to disclose to a member information about the fund's exposure to climate risks and how those risks are being managed.

Action step: Look for a fund that clearly discloses what it invests in, how it chooses those investments and how it values them. You will need to look well beyond the product disclosure statements to find this information. A tip to help you do this is to look for index funds where the index is named (for example, the ASX 200 for Australian shares) and which is implemented by investing in the individual constituent shares or bonds in the index. This is called 'full replication', and it means the constituents and their weighting are clear and on the public record. This may not be practical for fixed interest though, so if you can't find a full replication fund, a sampled or optimised fund is a close substitute. An alternative method of constructing an index fund (which you should avoid if possible) is to use derivatives (swaps, options and futures), which introduces additional risks and may conceal higher fees. Also, beware of index funds that include the word 'enhanced' in their name. This indicates some sort of proprietary approach, which is usually opaque.

Beware of unlisted assets

Most of the big funds have significant investments in unlisted assets (property, private equity and infrastructure) which lack the clarity and certainty of ongoing market-based valuation. In the absence of market transactions (which are infrequent), these investments are valued using financial models in a process managed by the custodian or fund manager. The methodology for these valuations is rarely disclosed. Unlisted assets also may be illiquid, especially in times of financial market stress.

The rules that govern how super funds classify their investments between growth and defensive mean that the reported growth/defensive split may not fully reflect the underlying assets. This makes it harder to assess performance. In theory, unlisted assets should deliver higher returns, but only if bought at the right price. Competition is intense for these investments, and it is unclear if this benefit actually flows through to retail investors. The greater transparency and liquidity of listed investments are therefore to be preferred in the absence of evidence to the contrary.

Action step: Look for investments in unlisted assets and avoid where possible.

Examine the fund's ownership

Many of Australia's largest super funds – 12 of the top 20 by assets – are operated on a 'profit for members' basis. This appears superficially seductive – no profit must mean higher returns, right? Not quite! We are used to this concept from cooperative businesses such as farmers' markets and bookstores. But super funds and investments are not bookstores, and the idea does not translate well.

Consider this: when you shop at a not-for-profit bookstore, you can compare each purchase at the time you make it. Once you've bought your book, it doesn't matter what happens to the bookstore that sold it to you. So, if an ill-judged investment and an inability to compete with Amazon leads to the collapse of a co-op bookstore, it has no effect on the books its customers have already purchased. It only means they have to buy future books elsewhere.

A super fund is different. You don't know the price until the end of the year – the expenses disclosed in the product disclosure statement (PDS) are just an estimate. And you don't know what performance you'll get until you actually get it. That's why the Australian Securities and Investments Commission (ASIC) makes funds include in their publications warnings such as, 'Past performance is not a reliable indicator of future performance'. Underperformance will only become evident after the fact, and there are significant tax and transaction costs involved in moving funds. It may also not be possible to replace insurance held through the fund if you move.

Profit is simply payment for risk. In a competitive market, there can be no excess return, so this will be the same as the economic cost of the risk. If you are not paying someone to take this risk, you are taking it yourself.

As well as the usual risks of operating a business, there are risks specific to funds management operations. These risks include overruns or delays in delivering IT systems, fines or penalties imposed by the regulator, marketing spend which does not generate the expected additional assets under management (AUM), unforeseen declines in AUM or member numbers, or unit pricing errors requiring compensation to affected members or former members. The effect of these risks is usually realised as either higher expenses or lower investment returns or paid for from reserves – in effect, member's money – and is quantifiable only in hindsight.

A 'for-profit' fund will usually have a suitably capitalised manager able to absorb these business risks and an incentive to preserve the value of their business, thus (in most cases) sheltering members from the risk. But in a 'profit for members' fund, the only place this risk can fall is on the members. So, any fine levied by ASIC on a fund will effectively fall on the very group of people the law was intended to protect. Recent changes to the law mean that funds will no longer be able to use members' investment balances to pay fines; however, it is not clear where else it could come from. A number of funds have sought to transfer money from reserves held for members (and included in the members' account balances – in other words, their retirement savings) to reserves held for the manager and so reduce the members' balances.

These risks are (usually) relatively small, and the fund's investment in the subsidiaries responsible for managing the investments, although not explicitly disclosed, is likely to be less than 1% of the fund's assets.

Overseas, some fund managers recognise this risk and have built a safety net mechanism. For example, Vanguard – the world's second-biggest fund manager by assets and owned by its US investors – caps the liability of investors at 0.4% of assets. No such cap is provided by any Australian super fund.

As a general rule, you should only accept risks if you are being rewarded for taking them. Accordingly, this risk should only be accepted by investors if there is a significant reduction in fees (all other things being equal) to compensate for taking this risk. In practice this is rarely the case.

Action step: Examine the ownership of the fund. If it is a member-owned (or 'profit for members') fund, ensure you are getting something in return. In most cases this will be lower fees – but in most cases this fee difference is inadequate. Do the numbers based on your balance.

See if the fund structure supports your investment choice

Not all funds are built the same way. Many of the differences are obscure (even to many lawyers) but can make a huge difference to your outcome. In some cases, they mean that you may not actually get the investment allocation you select.

For example, Hostplus invests via the Hostplus Pooled Super-annuation Trust, which in turn engages managers (some of which are owned by the trust) to actually invest. When you make a choice, Hostplus does not acquire an interest in the investment option you choose on your behalf. Instead, you are notionally invested in the nominated investment option. Hostplus predetermines the amount to be invested with any particular investment manager as part of their investment strategy. This introduces the risk of mismatch between the underlying assets and the investment options selected by Hostplus members. There is no disclosure as to how the notional return would be allocated in such a scenario.

Action step: Look for different or unusual structural features and assess what they mean for your future outcome. You will need to read quite a few PDSs. Look for differences – these will provide clues as to what might matter. The differences are likely to be hidden in vast slabs of common paragraphs, but it is worth persevering.

Check for fees

Now that you've got a short list of funds that deliver your required asset allocation with certainty and transparency, look at fees. You are now comparing apples with apples, and lower cost will generally win.

All funds charge fees; some fees are more evident than others. Generally, they consist of a fixed weekly or annual membership fee, an administration fee worked out as a percentage of your balance, and an investment management fee that is also based on your balance but dependent on which investment option you choose. There are also usually ad hoc fees for specific things such as changing your investment allocation.

Look carefully at any ongoing fees and fees that are deducted from your contributions. Don't focus too much on the fees that you're only going to incur occasionally, but be especially careful about fixed administration fees. These seemingly innocuous fees can be a material part of the total cost of your fund, especially if your balance is low. That $1.50 a week fee is 0.5% on a $15,600 balance and is not taken into account when reporting returns in most cases. Also, be wary of funds with unusually low fees. This may mean that the fee is not required to be disclosed, but just because it doesn't have to be disclosed doesn't mean it isn't eating away at your retirement savings. Identifying these fees can be hard.

Action step: Now that you've got a short list of broadly comparable funds, look at fees based on your balance. Funds are required to disclose the fees for a balance of $50,000. If your balance is different (as it will be in most cases), look at the fee for your balance.

Never let the insurance tail wag the super dog

Most super funds provide some level of insurance cover unless you choose to opt out. But is it the right cover for you? In most cases, the default cover will be insufficient or of inferior quality (as explained on page 100). For some people, however, the default insurance cover provided by their super fund might be the only cost-effective source of cover. This might be because of particular health issues or the type of work you do. If this applies to you, you may need to consider having two funds – one to provide the insurance you can't otherwise get, and one to meet your investment objectives. But you are not limited to the insurance provided by your super fund. You can now use your super to pay for insurance from a number of insurance providers.

Action step: Review your insurance needs. Check to see if you are better placed by choosing a policy outside your preferred fund. Only if you can't get cost-effective cover elsewhere should you allow this factor to influence your choice of fund.

Your super fund is your choice. Choose wisely.

Remember, everyone is different. Before you make your decision, decide what really matters. This will tell you how much importance to place on each of the eight items mentioned in this section of the book. This review may seem like a lot of hard work, and it is. But it matters, so it usually pays to seek professional advice.

How much is enough?

As a financial adviser, one of the toughest questions I'm asked is, 'How much super is enough?' It's tough because it involves trying to answer a whole bunch of questions about the world in up to 40 years' time. How much will you want to spend in retirement? How long do you plan on living? How much will you earn when you are 65? What will inflation and interest rates be doing then? These questions cannot be answered, and in any case, the human brain is not equipped to deal with events that might happen in 40 years.

The media and the finance industry typically claim you need $1 million to retire comfortably. This is based on work carried out by the Association of Superannuation Funds of Australia (ASFA), which styles itself as the peak industry body representing all super fund sectors, service providers and fund members. Each quarter, they publish a benchmark for the annual budget they say is required to fund either a comfortable or modest standard of living in retirement. In May 2021, this standard was $28,254 for a single person (or $40,829 for a couple) to support a modest lifestyle and $44,412 for a single person or ($62,828 for a couple) to support a comfortable lifestyle. The industry then took this number and said that to earn $40,829 (adjusted for inflation) until age 90, a couple needs to start with $1 million at age 65.

This ignores a number of important elements. A household after-tax income of $62,828 would put you in the top half of all Australian households by income. The median household income in December 2020 is $95,888 before tax. By age 65, you would expect to have your home paid off and your kids to have left home. So, your expenses should be less than the average household. You are likely to qualify for at least some age pension, which is currently $37,341 for a couple. And expenses in retirement don't tend to rise with inflation. Expenses tend to be higher at the beginning as people do the things they always planned to. They then fall as the desire and ability to spend declines, rising rapidly at the end as medical and accommodation bills escalate.

More importantly, this is of little help in assessing whether you are on track with your super savings unless you are close to retirement now.

A better way to think about what your retirement will cost is by taking a percentage of your final pay – 60% of this might be a better benchmark if you are a homeowner and have some assets outside super. Those who started work after the introduction of compulsory super will find that if they get the right advice early enough and look after their super (minimising fees and making sure it is properly invested), they will come close to this benchmark without additional payments.

The easiest way to check if you are on track is to frame your super balance as a number of months' (gross) pay. Grab your super fund statement and payslip. Divide your super fund balance by your gross monthly pay (before tax and excluding your super). So, if your super balance is $50,000 and you earn an annual salary of $60,000 (or $5,000 per month), your super fund balance represents ten months' pay.

At Life Sherpa we have developed a benchmark for how many months' pay you should have in your super fund at each stage of life, which you can view at www.lifesherpa.com.au/livethelife. Here's what it means in practice: a typical graduate starting out in the workforce in 2021 will earn a salary of around $50,000. Each month their employer will pay around $417 in super contributions. Each month the balance also earns an investment return. Over time, the contributions and the earnings really add up. By age 27, the balance should have reached six months' pay. Five years later, at age 32, the balance should be one year's pay. By age 33, the monthly earnings should exceed the monthly contributions. The effect of compounding is becoming visible. By age 40, you should have two years' pay, and five years' by age 55.

This will have you on track to have eight and a quarter years' pay by age 65, which should be capable of generating the equivalent of four months' pay with a high degree of certainty for 30 years or more. An income stream (pension) from your super account would be tax-free. By way of example, if you make $80,000 as a salary, you would take home just over $60,000 a year. Sixty per cent of this is $36,000. Eight and a quarter years' pay in super ($660,000) would buy a lifetime annuity of $26,763, tax-free and indexed to inflation. You could generate a higher return if you are prepared to accept some risk.

Now try it for yourself. How is your balance?

What happens when I die?

Your super usually represents a major part of your assets (your estate) if you die. Let's say you've got the right insurance and an up-to-date will. That's everything sorted for your family if you die, right? Not exactly! Your super is not dealt with in your will. So how do you make sure it goes where you want it to?

Your super balance (especially if you have life insurance in your super) and the family home form the bulk of the resources that will provide for your family. No tax is payable on the benefit if your recipient is a dependant – that is:

·   your spouse or former spouse (whether you are/were legally married or not)
·   your children (under 18) from a current or previous relationship, including adopted children and stepchildren (whether or not you were married to the other parent at the time)
·   anyone who was financially dependent on you before you died
·   someone with whom you were interdependent (for example, a carer who lived with you and you supported).

These benefits can be paid either as a lump sum or as a pension.

A super benefit paid to a non-dependant can only be paid as a lump sum and will be taxable. The portion that relates to contributions for which a tax deduction was not claimed will be tax free, and the balance will be taxed at 15%. Your super statement will usually identify the breakdown. If you only have employer contributions, it will all be taxable.

The trustee of your super fund decides what to do with your balance. Keep in mind that the trustee is usually a fund manager who doesn't know you personally – they are the issuer of the PDS you got when you signed up. If you have a self-managed super fund (SMSF), the trustee will be the remaining members of the fund or your personal representative.

Normally, the trustee decides to pay the amount to either one or more of your dependants or to your estate. If it gets paid to your estate, your executor will then allocate it according to your will. There are a few ways you can tell the trustee what you would like to happen to your super payout.

Most super funds let you make a binding nomination about what they should do. A valid binding nomination does not leave any discretion to the trustee. There are strict rules on how these nominations are made. Your super fund will usually have a special form with instructions on how to complete it. You need to update a binding nomination every three years or it will lapse. Some funds now offer non-lapsing death nominations that remain current until they are revoked or amended. You can only nominate a dependant or your estate. A binding nomination lets you set up your estate plan with more certainty.

A non-binding nomination is just a guide or suggestion to the trustee, who still retains the final say on how your super is distributed. The trustee usually focuses on your dependants (if any) at the time of your death. If you have dependants and nominate someone who doesn't depend on you, the trustee may not follow your wishes. A non-binding nomination provides greater flexibility.

Whatever you do, it is important to keep your nominations current and up to date with changes to your family circumstances – for example, if you marry, divorce or remarry, have children or your children turn 18. If you have no dependants, a binding nomination in favour of your estate will usually give you the control you need. You can deal with your super in your will.

For simple family circumstances – if you have dependent children and no children from previous relationships – a binding nomination in favour of the surviving partner or children, or both, is the usual way to go. It can often be beneficial to set this up as an income stream (pension). For more complex circumstances, such as blended families, families with adult children or dependent parents or siblings, and same-sex couples, professional advice is important.

Think about it today; tomorrow may be too late. Set aside some time every year to review your wishes in the light of any changes that have occurred.

Summary

- We need to make 40 years of income last for as much as 70 years of adult life. So, it's important to get the most out of your super.
- Drastically improve your retirement lifestyle by finding lost super, rounding up your super into one fund, and choosing the right find and investment option for you. Consider asset allocation, transparency, fund ownership, fund structure, fees and insurance.
- Determine if you are on track to accumulate enough super for your retirement by framing your super balance as a number of months' (gross) pay.
- Ensure your super will go where you want it to if you die.

Get your paperwork straight

This step is the 'make your bed first thing in the morning' of personal finance.

I remember my resistance to my mother's constant nagging to make my bed as a teenager. At the time, it seemed like a pointless exercise, because I knew I would simply toss it again when I returned to slumber each evening. As an adult, I can see the benefits in my own life – sorry Mum! But what really surprised me was the weight of evidence to support the benefits. Admiral William McRaven, a former Navy SEAL, explained why in a commencement speech he made to students at the University of Texas at Austin:

> 'If you make your bed every morning you will have accomplished the first task of the day. It will give you a small sense of pride and it will encourage you to do another task and another and another. By the end of the day, that one task completed will have turned into many tasks completed. Making your bed will also reinforce the fact that little things in life matter.'

So it is with keeping your paperwork straight. This simple task will relieve stress, make your life less complicated and even save you money.

Despite advances in technology, and a quick hurry-along from COVID-19, we still haven't become the paperless society envisioned over 30 years ago. Rather, we seem to be drowning in paper. So, what is the best way to sort out your paperwork and bills? How do you know what is important and how long you should keep it? The stress that clutter creates is avoidable, so my top tip to sort out your paper life is to develop a system. It doesn't matter what the system is. It has to be your system, but it is good if your partner knows where to find stuff, too – you never know when they will have to do it without you. A good system will follow this advice:

- Handle each piece of paper once.
- Open your paper mail next to the recycling bin so you can get rid of what's not important straight away. Shred anything with sensitive details.
- Split the rest into four piles: FILE, READ, PAY and DO. File anything in the FILE pile immediately; it gets a lot harder as the pile grows bigger. Keep your READ pile handy so you can deal with it when you get a spare moment.
- Schedule payments electronically and set a reminder a few days before the due date. This will remind you to make sure there are enough funds in the account.
- Schedule a time every year to cull what you don't need.
- Automate as much as possible.
- Go paperless. You can get most of your bills and statements electronically. Sign up for this wherever possible, but remember to download and save them somewhere that gets backed up. Most providers retain them only for a short period. Set up a reminder in your calendar (or choose automatic direct debit) so you don't overlook payment dates and face late fees.

- Keep your address details up to date with all companies you deal with.
- Keep an inventory of what you own and what you owe, and let someone know where it is. You never know when you might need them to do stuff if you can't.
- Dump it when it's no longer needed. I have been an inveterate hoarder when it comes to paper. I discovered the cathartic effect of dumping when I needed to deal with the contents of our family home when it was sold following my divorce. Out went decades of credit card statements (I had kept every statement since I left university), utility bills, and bank and investment statements. The pile eventually filled several wheelie bins, but boy did I feel better.

The trick with that last point is knowing what you need to keep and for how long. Here's my recommendation:

- **Job-related paperwork:** Keep your job application, letter of offer, any arrangements as to how you will be paid and performance reviews for as long as you work for that organisation. Dump these when you're one year into your next job. Keep payslips for the current year until you get your annual payment summary. Dump all but the last two monthly payslips (and always keep at least three on file).
- **Your finances:** Keep bank and credit card statements for as long as you have physical room for them (and at least the period required for tax). Credit card statements are great support if you have an insurance claim for a burglary. Electronic statements make this much easier. Keep your application form, offer documents, the product disclosure statement or brochure, and any advice you received in relation to any financial product you buy (share, super fund, investment or insurance). Dump when the product has expired.

- **Your assets:** Keep receipts for any major asset (your car, boat or anything of value), together with a photo and any proof of ownership. If the receipt is on thermal paper that is likely to fade, take a photo of the receipt with your phone or make a photocopy. Dump when you no longer own the asset.

- **Your home:** Keep a file on your purchase (agent's flyer, purchase contract, settlement advice) and your loan (your loan application, advice from your broker, loan offer documents, your copy of the loan agreement and mortgage, and every loan statement). Keep for the life of the loan. Keep rates, water, electricity, gas and repair bills. If you ever rent out your home, these bills can help reduce your future capital gains tax (CGT). That's because the costs of owning an asset (for which you aren't able to claim a tax deduction, mostly because you incurred them when the asset wasn't generating assessable income) will be added to your cost base for CGT purposes when working out how much of the sale price of the home is a taxable gain. Keep for as long as you own your home.

- **Tax:** According to the ATO, you must keep written evidence of expenses and other deductions for five years from when you lodge your tax return or, if you have a dispute with the ATO, five years from when that dispute was resolved. This includes the return itself, any calculations you made to get to the numbers on the form and documents supporting those numbers, including your payment summary, bank statements, dividend and interest statements, share certificates (CHESS Statements) and contract notes, receipts or credit card statements for work-related expenses, your logbook for your car and receipts for expenses, warranties and user manuals (keep these together, and when you sell, replace or dump the item, do the same with the instructions and warranty), and passwords and usernames.

One of the best ways to save sensitive information such as passwords and usernames is offline. Keep a dedicated notebook for this purpose, and list all your usernames and passwords. Share this with one person you trust – a person who might need them too. Keep this book or file in a safe place where you can access it easily. Alternatively, use a password manager such as LastPass, Dashlane or, if you are a little handier when it comes to IT matters, Bitwarden.

Very important paperwork

Perhaps the three most important pieces of paper – yes, in this electronic age, these still have to be on paper – are your will, an enduring power of attorney and an advance care directive (often called a 'living will').

Where there's a will...

Everyone over the age of 18 who owns anything of value should have a will. A will is a legal document that details how you want the things you own to be distributed when you die. Wills aren't just for older people with money and complex family situations. When you turn 18 and start accumulating things and relationships, it's already a good time to arrange one. By making a will, you remove the doubts and difficulties that can arise when there is no evidence of your final wishes.

A will allows you to appoint a person you trust to carry out your instructions (your executor), helps provide for the people you care about, allows you to provide for your pets, lets you specify who is to get particular things you own, lets you leave instructions for your funeral arrangements and allows you to make a gift to charity. Wills are often not really about the money; they are more about making sure that the most appropriate person gets to keep sentimental items such as art, collectables, letters and photos.

When you die, your money and possessions are known as your 'estate'. If you die without a valid will, you won't have any say about how your estate is distributed. This is known as 'dying intestate'. The law sets out rules for allocating your things, which could be very different from what you want to happen. The rules vary from state to state, but some or all of your estate could end up in the hands of the government.

Dying intestate can also cause complications, delays and extra costs for those you leave behind. For example, the assets of someone who dies intestate in NSW are distributed this way:

· firstly to their spouse and any children
· if none, then their parents
· if none, then their siblings
· if none, then their grandparents
· if none, then their aunts and uncles
· if none, then their first cousins.

If there are none of these, then the government gets it all, although a second cousin, close friend or charity who believes you might have left them something can apply for a share in your estate.

Anyone over 18 can make a will as long as they have the mental capacity to be aware of what they are doing. Making a will can be a straightforward process and doesn't have to cost a lot of money. It's simply a matter of expressing your wishes clearly and planning for what you want to happen if the person you wish to leave something to dies before you do. It's essential to be very clear and follow the rules carefully to avoid arguments over who gets what.

You can buy a kit at a post office or legal stationers, but it is safer to have a solicitor or trustee company do your will for you. If you have dependent children, you should get a professional to advise on tax issues (such as the benefits of a testamentary trust).

Your will must be in writing and signed by you in the presence of two or more witnesses, who must all be present at the same time. Your witnesses must also sign the will in your presence. A beneficiary under a will should not be a witness or they may lose their entitlement under the will.

You can choose anyone over 18 to be an executor; most people nominate a trusted friend or family member (usually one of the beneficiaries). There is a lot of paperwork involved, however, so it may help to appoint a lawyer or trustee company. If you don't name one, the court will appoint an administrator after you die.

Death duties were abolished in Queensland in 1979, followed closely by the other states. This means that, in most cases, someone inheriting your assets will not pay tax when they receive it. There are a couple of traps to watch out for, though. If the person who receives your super was not a dependant – primarily a child under 18, spouse, former spouse or other person who depended on you because they were otherwise unable to meet their basic daily necessities – the amount will be subject to tax of up to 30%. For any other asset, although no tax is payable at the time of inheritance, there may be a later liability.

The person who inherits an asset which they later sell will need to pay CGT at the time they sell, based on the difference between the original purchase price (paid by the deceased) and the sale price. However, there are a few exceptions to this. There is a two-year grace period during which no tax would be payable on a sale if the asset was the principal residence of the deceased before their death. Also, if the deceased acquired the asset before 1986, the relevant value for determining the gain is the value at death, not the value when originally acquired.

You may wish to think about balancing out the after-tax benefit if you are splitting assets with different tax treatments between a number of beneficiaries. You should get professional advice on this if the amount is material.

A will made in another country, and valid in that country, will be accepted in NSW and most other Australian states. If it is not written in English, you will need a certified translation into English when the time comes.

You can change your mind about the contents of your will at any time, but you can't just cross out clauses or write in new ones. The way to update your will is to add a codicil or draft a new one. A codicil is a document prepared like a will that sets out the changes you want.

Your will lasts until you die, unless you change it, make a new one or revoke (cancel) it. Getting married after making your will revokes the old one. Divorce revokes the parts of your will that refer to your ex-partner. Don't bet on this last point, though – don't rely on the partial revocation of your will that occurs when you divorce. Write a new will. You should also get legal advice about how to update your will if your circumstances change – for example, you marry, divorce, have children or grandchildren, or your partner dies.

Your will should be easy to find after you die. If it can't be found, the court can presume you destroyed it and deem you to have died intestate. Keep the original in a safe place (with your bank, lawyer or trustee company), but not so safe that nobody can find it! Keep a copy at home among your personal papers with a note saying where to find the original. You should also tell your executor where you have put the original.

The money in your super fund isn't part of your estate and will be dealt with differently. It is also the only part of your estate that will be taxed when you die. As I mentioned earlier, if anyone who is not a dependant inherits your super it will be taxed. If you don't specify who will receive your super, the trustee of your super fund (usually a fund manager who doesn't know you personally) will decide. They will usually focus on the needs of your dependants. You can, however, leave them instructions (see Step 5).

Enduring power of attorney

A will can only deal with what happens if you die, but it's what happens when you are alive and unable to make decisions yourself that can create the biggest problems. Do you know who would make your decisions for you if you became incapacitated?

In the same way that income protection is a higher priority than life insurance, what happens if you can't look after your money or health is a higher priority than having a will. If you want someone to look after your finances in the event you are unable to do this yourself, you need to appoint a power of attorney. The rules on this vary a little from state to state.

A power of attorney enables you (the principal) to authorise someone else (your attorney) to carry out financial transactions on your behalf. You must have mental capacity to understand what you are doing when you make the power. A standard or general power of attorney will cease to have effect if you lose your mental capacity. If you want it to continue after you lose your mental capacity, you will need an enduring power of attorney. There are some subtle differences in the drafting and signing requirements. An enduring power must have your signature witnessed by a prescribed person, such as a solicitor, barrister, registrar of the local court or a licensed conveyancer.

Appoint someone you trust, and someone willing and able to act when the time comes. In effect, your attorney gets to act as if they were you, so make sure you know and trust them well.

Even if you have someone you really trust, there are a few things you can do to add further protection to prevent the power of attorney being misused. One is to ask your solicitor (or someone else you trust) to retain the power of attorney document, so the attorney has to convince them that what they intend to do is appropriate. Another is to appoint more than one person jointly, so they both have to agree before they can do anything using your power of attorney.

If the attorney needs to deal with real estate, the power will need to be registered with the land titles office in the relevant state or territory. This doesn't have to be done until the time comes to use it.

A power of attorney deals only with money matters. In NSW, the Guardianship Act allows you to appoint someone to make decisions on your behalf about things such as where you will live and what health care you want, and to consent to medical or dental treatment. Other states have broadly similar arrangements. A guardianship only becomes operative if you are unable to make decisions yourself. Both the person making the appointment and the guardian must sign an appointment of enduring guardian form, and it must be witnessed by an Australian solicitor or barrister, the registrar of the local court, or an overseas-registered foreign lawyer.

Advance care directives

You can leave instructions for your guardian or attorney or others about your future medical treatment should you become incapacitated. You might, for example, specify what measures are or are not to be taken to prolong your life.

Although such documents are often called 'living wills', they are not legally binding and have nothing to do with your normal will. They are more accurately called 'advance care directives' and are important guides to help those who need to decide what to do when you can't. You need to be sure that whoever you nominate knows your wishes, and you are confident they will be comfortable carrying them out.

If you are a parent of young children, or older children who are unable to look after themselves because of disability, you should also think about how they will be cared for if you can't care for them, either because you die or become incapacitated. This is usually done via a clause in your will that expresses your wishes for their future care and support, such as: 'I request X to be the guardian to assist, support and care for my daughter/son for the remainder of her/his life or until they turn [age] years old'. These clauses are not legally binding, but they provide an indication of your wishes for your family left behind, and they can be very important if your estate is contested in court or a guardianship or financial management application comes before a tribunal, panel, board or court. Usually, you would specify what portion of your estate is to be available to the guardian to meet the costs.

Talk to the person you intend to nominate first.

Summary

- Develop a system for dealing with your paperwork. It doesn't matter what the system is, only that it exists and is followed.
- The three most important pieces of paper are your will, an enduring power of attorney and an advance care directive. Make sure to set these up.

Step 7

Buy and pay off your home

Australians love their homes. Not only do we have one of the highest rates of home ownership in the world, and live in homes that are among the biggest in the world, we have the lowest home loan default rates in the world. Buying their first home is an important rite of passage for most Australians. We also have a very high number of people who own a second property that is rented out. Statistics from the ATO show that almost 2.3 million Australians declared rental income on their tax returns.

As I noted in the introduction, house prices have risen rapidly over the past 30 years, driven largely by falling interest rates, more flexible lending standards and the increase in dual-income households. These three factors alone account for most of the increase in house prices over the period. It is difficult to see what other factors could give the same boost to housing prices over the next 30 years, particularly with slowing income growth and the likelihood of rising interest rates as they return to some sort of normality. Does this mean now is not a good time to be buying property? No, it doesn't! The golden rule is to buy property, but not too much, and only when the time is right for you.

As a financial planner, the question people most often ask me is whether they should rent or buy their home. It's one of the most difficult questions to answer definitively. It's the ultimate 'it depends' question! When people ask this question, they are usually thinking of this as an investment decision. And when it comes to your own home, this is usually the wrong way of looking at it. It is better looked at as a risk management decision.

Let me explain. We all need somewhere to live. By this I mean a safe, secure roof over our heads that meets our needs and those of our families. This is a lifelong commitment that never goes away. We can choose to acquire this on the short-term market by renting. This way we pay the market rate, whatever that might be at the time. I call this the variable option. Alternatively, we can choose to fix the price we pay by buying a property. (In some countries, long-term fixed rentals are available, which would provide a valid third option.)

In Australia, the cash cost of renting, at least in the short term, has almost always been lower than the ongoing cost of buying. There are three main drivers of this.

First, there are significant transaction costs involved in buying and selling real estate. For buyers the main cost is stamp duty, which, for example, would be $18,000 for a $500,000 property in NSW. This is the equivalent of nine months' rent.

Second, the rental cost is usually less than the cost of borrowing the money required to buy the property, or the income that is forgone because this money could not be invested elsewhere. The rental yield (annual rent divided by the market value of the property) in Australian capital cities has historically been around 5%, or roughly $1 per week for each $1000 the property is worth. This means that a $500,000 property will usually rent for around $500 per week or less.

The standard variable home loan interest rate has been above 5% for most of the past 50 years, although rates below this are available at the time of writing.

Third, homeowners incur a number of expenses that renters don't. These include rates, maintenance, strata levies and building insurance.

Over time, however, inflation helps push up all of the costs other than the amount the owner has spent to purchase the property, so that at some point the renter's cash cost starts to exceed the owner's cash cost. This phenomenon, whereby an initially higher cost to buy is slowly whittled away by inflation, means that given a long enough time period, buying will work out cheaper. How long that period will be is the great unknown. As the famous economist John Maynard Keynes said, 'In the long run we are all dead'.

In practice, buying delivers certainty and a bunch of intangible benefits. The question for you then should be, 'Is now the right time for me to choose certainty at the expense of flexibility, knowing it will cost me a little more right now?'

There are some circumstances in which the fixed option will almost always be more expensive – for example, if you need to move homes in a short period (usually any period less than five years). In such cases, the transaction costs and increased expenses almost always outweigh the benefits of fixing the costs of housing. On the other hand, over any long period (usually ten years or more) over the past 50 years, the fixed option has worked out cheaper.

But what about the gain (or loss) in the value of the property? This is somewhat academic, because the value of any alternative property is likely to have risen (or fallen) by the same amount, so the increase in wealth can never be realised for so long as you need somewhere to live. Similarly, any loss can be deferred, so long as you can keep up your mortgage payments and don't need to move. The wealth effect, whereby we feel richer because the value of our homes has gone up, can also encourage us to spend more of our incomes. This can quietly whittle away much of the advantage. And don't forget we could have invested the difference in cash cost between renting and buying, which could have made us more or less than the increase in the value of the property.

Nevertheless, home ownership creates discipline around saving, provides a store of wealth that can be accessed, is favourably treated by our tax and welfare systems, and improves your credit rating, which can lead to lower borrowing costs in future. The homeowner also gets the benefit of fixed housing costs and all of the psychological benefits of home ownership. These should not be underestimated.

Ultimately, choosing between renting and buying is a very personal decision. In my view, the key is buying the right amount of house with a cost that allows you to sit tight through thick and thin (I'll show you how to work this out later). Oh, and don't move for a long time!

How you pay for the house raises several other issues. By borrowing money to fund the purchase, you are exchanging one risk (variable housing costs) for another (variable funding costs). To some extent, this can be managed by taking out a fixed-rate loan, but we don't have access to long-term fixed-rate loans in Australia as they do in the US and other markets. More on this later.

There is a third option that shouldn't be forgotten and is becoming popular among young Australians: rent where you live and buy an investment property elsewhere. This is often referred to as 'rentvesting', and I'll cover this in more detail at the end of this chapter.

Get into financial shape first

Getting into shape to buy your home or investment property starts long before you start to give up every Saturday morning to go house hunting. Here are six important actions to take before you start.

Check your credit report

Your most important asset in the property hunt is a clean credit report. If you haven't read yours in a while – or ever – now is the time to do it. You can get your credit report free of charge once a year. There are three main providers: Equifax, illion and Experian.

When you get your credit report, you need to check the following things:

1. Are your personal details correct? Check your full name, address, employers (past and present) and driver's licence details.
2. Are there any credit queries you don't recognise? Banks and credit card companies make an enquiry every time you apply for credit. Too many can reduce your ability to borrow. Some credit providers (American Express and Citibank in particular) do regular checks on existing cardholders – these are nothing to worry about.
3. Are there any judgements or payment defaults? These are potential showstoppers. Are they correct? Is there a reason?
4. If you are a director of a company, this is usually listed too, as well as enquiries about you as a director; check the list is correct and up to date.

Once you have the information, you can do something about it. If there are any errors (something that is factually incorrect), write to the relevant credit reporting body and request that they correct it. (They will have a form on their website.) If there are any defaults, contact the provider and see if you can make a deal to repay some or all of the outstanding amount and they will amend the listing.

There are a lot of companies that claim to be able to repair impaired credit. These should be treated with extreme caution. Most of what they claim to do, you can do yourself, although they will have more detailed knowledge of the rules that lenders must follow before lodging a default and so can identify sloppy paperwork that could mean the report has to be withdrawn. They're not miracle workers – if there is a real default, they can't just make it go away if the lender has followed the rules.

Time will heal a lot. Over time, the significance of a default diminishes, and most disappear from your report after five to ten years depending on the default.

Close your unused credit cards

When a lender assesses your loan application, they generally work on the assumption that your credit limits are fully drawn and count the minimum payment as an expense. So, if you earn $80,000 and have a credit card limit of $5000, you could borrow $505,000. But increase your credit card limit to $10,000 and your borrowing limit falls to $484,000. That $5000 increased limit has reduced your borrowing capacity by $21,000. Every dollar of credit card limit reduces your ability to borrow by roughly $4 to $5.

If you're not using a card, get rid of it. The same goes for store cards. You will usually need to provide the bank with statements for your accounts showing all transactions over at least a 12-month period. Get into the habit of making all payments on time, in full. Late payments work against you. Get all of your accounts up to date and operating within their limits.

No more credit applications

Think twice about applying for credit in the year leading up to your mortgage application. If you intend to use 0% balance transfer offers to reduce your debts, do it well in advance. If you want to take advantage of interest-free loans from furniture providers, wait until after your loan has settled.

Stay put

Moving house or jobs frequently can create issues in getting a loan approved. Banks like to see stability, with at least six months in a job and any probation period completed. If you are self-employed, a two-year track record is important. If you rent, it is best to go through an estate agent, so you can show a proper lease and an extract of the rent ledger to demonstrate you have paid the rent on time every time.

Gather your supporting documents

A fair bit of documentation is required to verify all the information the bank needs to approve your loan. Start a file for the documents you need, so you're ready when the time comes.

Get saving

Open a bank account and put some money away each month. If your parents are going to give you a helping hand, it helps if you have the money in an account in your name for more than three months. A good savings record is necessary to demonstrate 'genuine savings'.

How much deposit do I need?

Your parents and many professional advisers would recommend at least a 20% deposit on a home purchase. When you add in the obvious costs such as stamp duty, legal fees and the cost of building inspections and conveyancing, the amount you need to get to 20% really adds up. Then you have to factor in the more obscure costs, such as replacing the locks in your new home and – the one that catches out a lot of people – the adjustments made on settlement. These relate to expenses such as rates, land tax and utilities charges that have been paid by the previous owner but relate to the period after you take over. These are pro-rated on settlement. For example, you may be expecting rates to be paid quarterly and then find that the previous owner has paid the full year's rates, leaving you with a bigger bill than you expected. Then there are always minor (or not so minor) repairs to be done at the new house that you may not have spotted in your inspection. There can also be costs to clean your old rental and fix up any damage so you can get your bond back.

It can really add up. For example, a $500,000 home purchase in NSW will trigger about $17,707 in government charges (mainly stamp duty). Throw in a further $3295 in costs for inspections and conveyancing, on top of a 20% deposit, and you're up for $121,002. This is a big sum of money to get together. However, a couple with a pre-tax household income of $125,000 would be able to get this together in a little over six years by allocating all of the Grow portion of their 50/30/20 budget ($20,000) to this.

So, what's magic about 20%? It's all about the loan to value ratio (LVR). This is the ratio of the value of the property to the amount of the loan. This means that if you want to buy a property with a purchase price of $500,000 and you need to borrow $450,000, your LVR is $450,000 divided by $500,000 (or 90%).

As the LVR rises, so does the risk to the lender. As far as most lenders are concerned, the critical LVR is 80%. The magic 20% is simply 100% minus 80%. If you want to borrow more than this, they will usually insist you pay for lenders mortgage insurance (LMI). This is a one-off charge that can amount to thousands of dollars, but it can usually be added onto your loan.

LMI protects the lender from losses in the event that you default on your home loan. It covers the lender for the difference between what they get when they sell your property and the amount you still owe them. The LMI provider will then seek to recover this from you.

LMI should not be confused with mortgage protection insurance, which helps pay your home loan payments if you can't due to illness or unemployment.

In practice, LMI means you can get into your own home sooner with a smaller deposit.

Table 4 shows the costs involved in buying and funding a $500,000 property in NSW at different levels of savings. The total cost of purchase, excluding LMI, is $521,002; this consists of the purchase price ($500,000), stamp duty ($17,707) and other costs ($3295).

Table 4: Costs for purchasing a $500,000 property in NSW

	Scenario 1	Scenario 2	Scenario 3	Scenario 4
Your cash savings	$50,702	$59,102	$70,952	$121,002
LMI	$17,480	$8,820	$4887.50	$0
Loan	$485,025	$474,984	$461,331	$400,000
LVR	97%	90%	85%	80%
Total upfront cost	$538,482	$529,882	$525,889.50	$521,002
Typical rates	3.59% variable	1.99% fixed	1.99% fixed	1.85% fixed
Monthly repayments	$2203	$1754	$1703	$1449

This means that the minimum practical savings required for this property is $50,702 (of which at least $25,000 would need to be genuine savings as defined by the banks). This would mean that your LVR on settlement would be 97%. An extra $8400 in savings would reduce the LMI, reduce your interest rate and give you greater choice of lenders.

It may be possible to reduce how much of this you have to save yourself by accessing some of the incentives available. In NSW for example, a $10,000 grant is available if you buy a new home worth no more than $750,000. First home buyers are also exempt from stamp duty if they buy an existing home for less than $650,000 or a new home for less than $800,000. This would reduce the cash required by $17,707. A partial exemption is available up to $800,000 for an existing home and $1 million for a new home.

Using the Life Sherpa rule of thumb of buying a property worth no more than five to six times your gross income, you should have a gross household income of $83,000 to $100,000 to buy this ($500,000) home. For example, if both people in a couple earned $50,000, they would have a combined gross income of $100,000 and a net income of $84,400 after tax. The monthly payments on a $400,000 loan, given the interest rates at time of writing, would be $1449, or 20% of their net income. This fits within the 50/30/20 rule, as it leaves them 29.4% to pay for the rest of their Chore expenses. Bear in mind though that interest rates are at historic lows and are likely to rise.

When you see the price of LMI, it can be tempting to try to minimise it by gathering every dollar you can to maximise your deposit, including your emergency stash. While this may be instinctive, it can be very risky. Maintaining an emergency stash is a key foundation of the Life Sherpa way to reduce financial stress. It is important because it gives your finances resilience to cope with unexpected events or loss of income. The likelihood of unexpected expenses increases substantially when you become a homeowner. At the same time, the impact of losing your job increases dramatically. This is the time you really need an emergency stash. In fact, it is probably a good time to increase the number of months' expenses you keep on hand.

The one exception to this rule is if you are close to an LMI pricing threshold. LMI is priced as a percentage of the loan amount. The percentage rises as the LVR rises, but it rises in steps. For example, the rate applicable for all loans between 88.01% and 90% is the same, but step up to 90.1% and the rate increases dramatically. Therefore, the difference between borrowing $449,000 and $451,000 could be quite large. In these circumstances, you could consider drawing $2000 from your emergency stash, as long as you have a plan to replenish it soon.

How much loan can I afford?

The secret to riding out the ups and downs of the housing market is to make sure you can keep up with the payments on your home loan. This means you will not be forced to sell when the market is down or before you are ready. The easiest way to do this is to make sure your payments fit the 50/30/20 rule.

In Step 1, I described how your budget should be split 50/30/20 on average: up to 50% of your take-home pay is allocated to Chore expenses (housing, utilities, transport, clothing and food), 30% to Live expenses (fun stuff) and 20% to Grow expenses (goals). Usually this means you will need to keep your loan to less than five times your gross annual salary. Add in your deposit and you are looking at a property worth just less than six times your income. For couples, if that is five times both of your incomes, think about whether you will want to drop back to one income later and the impact that might have on your budget.

If your Chore expenses are getting close to 60% of your income because of the size of your home loan, think about what else you are prepared to sacrifice from your Live and Grow expenses, and think about how any changes to your income or expenditure in the near future might affect your situation. This is your number-one risk reduction strategy. It is far more important than the size of your deposit. Banks will generally agree to lend you more than you can comfortably repay, which can really get in the way of the lifestyle you truly want.

Most lenders use an assumption of living costs – the Household Expenditure Measure (HEM), developed by the Melbourne Institute in 2011 – in order to decide how much of your income they are happy for you to allocate to paying for your home loan. This will usually place a ceiling on how much you can borrow regardless of how frugal you are. But in practice, it usually means that if you borrow as much as the bank is prepared to lend for your home, you are likely to be condemning yourself to a very modest lifestyle for a considerable period. Using this assumption, a single person earning $80,000 annually would take home $5161 each month after tax. Payments on the $622,000 loan a lender could approve (at a variable rate of 2.24%) would be $2375, or 46% of the total take-home pay.

The bank's obligation is to lend you no more than you can repay without undue hardship. Your objective is to buy the home you need and live the life you want with the money you have. Just because the bank will lend a sum of money to you doesn't mean you can comfortably afford to repay it.

Try living on what you would have left if you were making your mortgage repayments. Work out how much the repayment on your planned loan would be, add in the additional costs of being a home-owner (strata fees, rates, insurance, and repairs and maintenance) and then deduct what you are paying in rent now. Put this amount away each month so you can experience what it would be like to live with this loan. Do you still have the money to do the things you want to? Does this feel restrictive? If it does, are you happy with the trade-offs you have to make? Remember, with low inflation, it could take a while before your pay increases enough to remove the restrictions on your lifestyle and bring your budget back into balance.

What to buy

Once you know how much you can really afford, work out what you need. Make a checklist of the features that are important to you. This will save you time later by focusing your search and allowing you to avoid wasting time visiting properties that would never suit. It will also help make inspections more productive.

This checklist shouldn't just be a list of features: it should be a comprehensive guide to all the trade-offs you're going to have to make. It will help you to quickly get to 'No' and to know when you've found the right property.

Start your checklist by listing all the things you're looking for in a property. Include the obvious stuff, such as the number of bedrooms, the size and layout of the kitchen, and number of bathrooms, toilets, car spaces and so on. Are you looking for a fixer-upper or do you want the hard work already done? Add the less tangible aspects, such as location, amenities, schools, access to public transport. Try to create your list using positive attributes. This will make the 'why' clearer when it comes to making trade-offs. For example, you might list 'a quiet location next to a park' rather than 'not on a busy main road'.

Now for the important bit: prioritise! Rank each entry on your list for importance. Is it a deal-breaker or just a nice-to-have? Categorise each entry as either:

1. a must-have ('I am simply not prepared to buy a property without this feature, or the ability to easily add it, at any price')
2. a nice-to-have ('I would like to have it and I'm prepared to pay more for it')

3. a would-be-good ('I would like it, but I'm not prepared to pay more for it').

Consider the trade-offs you are prepared to make. Is a big yard more or less important than a car space? Do the kids really need a bedroom each? Are you prepared to trade size for location and distance to work?

Being absolutely sure about what is important to you is the key to avoiding the curse of too much house. The biggest cause of money stress I see is spending too much of the family budget on the house. Not only does the house itself eat up a large chunk of your budget, it also drives up other costs – for example, where you shop, where you eat and where your kids go to school are all a function of where you live and can have a huge impact on your cost of living.

Once you've got this clear in your mind, you can identify the suburbs that are likely to be able to deliver what you want at a price that fits comfortably within your budget.

Limiting your search to just a few key suburbs will make your life easier and cut down on the number of Saturday mornings you'll need to sacrifice. It will also allow you to quickly develop a sense of what your budget will get you, so you don't waste so much time looking at properties that will sell above your maximum. Go to lots of auctions and keep on top of sales results. A good agent will keep you informed.

Use your checklist to select the properties to visit and to document your inspections. The secret to getting the most out of open houses and surviving the great property hunt is adopting a systematic approach to your search.

It may be the biggest purchase most of us will ever make, but usually we only have a few chances to visit a property before making an offer. That's why it's so important to take your time. Don't rush your visits. Look carefully. Think carefully. Really take in what is on offer. This is where your checklist will help ensure you don't overlook something important.

Check that the appliances work; turn on the taps; flush the toilet. Observe the water pressure and the time it takes for the hot water to reach the tap, and notice any noises in the pipework. Check the electricity: do the switches, power points and fuse box look new and clean with modern circuit breakers, or do they still have bakelite fittings?

Look past the superficial styling at the underlying fabric of the home. Sellers are increasingly using stylists, which can often distract you from looking properly at the house itself. Smart furniture placement can make rooms seem larger and hide a multitude of sins. Take a measuring tape and make time to put it to work. Measure rooms, open cupboard doors, check storage space and look behind the sofa to see if the walls are OK.

Check that window and door locks are secure. What do the garden and exterior look like? Is it safe for your dogs or children? Check out the parking. Will your car fit? What are the access and turning circle like?

Use your phone to take pictures. This will help clear away the blur after a day's inspections. After a while, it can be really difficult to differentiate one property from another. Make notes about all the things you liked and didn't like about a property. How does it compare to what else you've seen? When you get home, you can go back over your notes in your own time and decide which properties deserve a second look. Pay particular attention to faults and defects – these will stop you falling in love with the property and help give you bargaining power on price.

Ask plenty of questions. You won't always get a full and honest answer; after all, the agent works for the seller, not you, and they are singularly focused on getting a sale. Keeping that in mind, talk with the real estate agent, ask as many questions as you can and keep notes on the answers. Often what they don't say is just as important as what they do say. Most won't actually lie, but they will present the property in the best light – they only get paid when they get a sale.

Here are some questions to ask at your next inspection:

- Have there been any offers on the property?
- Why were they rejected?
- How long has the property been for sale?
- Has there been a building or pest inspection done?
- Why are the owners selling? (If the sale is the result of a divorce or a deceased estate, you might just snag a bargain.)
- When was the house last renovated?
- How old is the plumbing and wiring? What about the appliances, the heating system and the hot water service?

Get to know the local agents. Get them onside. Let them know you are a serious buyer, but be careful not to let them know how much you're really prepared to pay. It's usually best to downplay a little, but be realistic. Make sure they have your details so they can let you know when new properties are about to come on the market.

If you visit a property and you conclude it's not for you, let the agent know. This gives them a better sense of what you are looking for and they will let you know about new listings, potentially putting you ahead of others when it comes to finding your dream home.

New or old?

As the advertising jingle goes, there's nothing like living in a brand-new home. This is often a matter of personal preference, particularly when it comes to your own home. As a financial planner, I'm often asked whether it is better to buy a new property or an older property when it comes to property investment.

New property will usually need less maintenance and may be covered by a warranty. If you're time-poor or just not interested or skilled in maintenance, then new is a good option for you. Newer properties are also usually designed to maximise light and space and are often close to employment areas or transport links, so they can be attractive places to live, easier to rent out and command higher rents. For investors, they usually offer higher or longer depreciation benefits, which can create tax benefits to help with cash flow.

Proponents of off-the-plan purchases, many of whom have a vested interest in the commissions they generate, make the following arguments:

- You might get a better price because developers need to presell a proportion of the apartments they build in order to secure bank funding, and time is money for them. Also, you buy tomorrow at today's price. It can be 18 months or more between signing up and settling. This means that in a rising market, you can secure a property at today's prices and benefit from any capital growth in the market before you settle. (In most cases, developers and agents try to anticipate this and seek to charge more than today's price – but this means you also run the risk of the values being lower on completion than at presale time.)
- Buying off the plan can save you stamp duty. In some states, such as Victoria, you will generally pay stamp duty only on the land value, not on the whole purchase price. This saving can really add up.
- Many of the government incentives for first-home buyers are limited to purchasers of new properties or provide them with bigger incentives. In NSW for example, first-home buyers get a $10,000 grant for buying a newly built property worth less than $750,000. There are also stamp duty exemptions available

for new properties worth less than $1 million (as opposed to $800,000 for established properties).

- Time is on your side. When you buy off the plan, you get more time to get your finances together, save more and to sell your existing property.
- You may have a bigger choice. Usually, when you buy off the plan, you will have a range of properties to choose from. So, if you act quickly and are prepared to commit early, you may be able to pick a better property. Maybe you could get a better position, aspect or floor layout. This can give you an advantage when it comes to rental or resale.

Despite these arguments, my general advice is to avoid brand-new properties – especially when this means buying off the plan, which introduces a whole range of risks. You can get most of the benefits of new properties at a more attractive price by buying resales after a few years.

Why do I take this view?

- We live in a two-tier market. Foreign buyers are generally limited to buying new properties. They make up a significant proportion of the buyers for new stock, especially in the inner city and high-density markets, and they won't be there to buy your property when you come to sell it.
- New properties often cost more than older properties in the same area.
- Banks don't like them and will usually lend a lower percentage of the purchase price, meaning you will have to find a bigger deposit. You also won't know precisely how much you can borrow until completion.

- They may be different to the rest of the housing stock in the local area, so may not offer the things that have attracted people to the area in the first place.
- There are likely to be a few very similar properties being sold at the same time if the property is located in a brand-new development. A few hasty resales can affect the values of all the properties in the immediate area.
- If it is a multi-stage development, some of which can take a decade or more, if you wish to sell you will be competing against the new stock, so you may not get as good a price.
- There's not much scope to add value by renovating or extending – the developer has already done all the work, and any more work could see you overcapitalising.
- Contracts for off-the-plan properties are usually lengthy, generally favour the developer and can be extremely complex. You will need a good lawyer, who will usually charge more than they would for a simple conveyance of an established property.
- You don't really know what you are getting. All you have to judge what the property will look like is the display suite, architect's impressions, finishes schedules and floor plans. It's tough, and often the finished product is quite different. Off-the-plan contracts generally provide for some variations in the floor area, fixtures and fittings.
- You may not get your property when you want it. Delays happen in construction all the time. Sometimes these can be lengthy – years, even. Approvals may be delayed. Weather could slow things down. The builder could go out of business. Financing for the project may be delayed or cancelled. If any of this happens, your deposit will be tied up and you won't have your property. Most off-the-plan contracts favour the developer and their financiers. There is usually a lengthy period (called the 'sunset date') before you will have any rights to cancel the contract due to delay.

Additionally, older properties have the following advantages:

- There is usually less price fluctuation than with new properties in the same area.
- You can add value by renovating, extending, subdividing and developing.
- Older properties are often situated on larger blocks, which can often help drive property values upwards.
- You are more likely to be buying at 'true' market value, with no profit margin set by the seller.
- They are more prevalent in well-established suburbs that can demonstrate consistent growth.

Getting your loan together

Getting a home loan is easier than it was in your parents' day, but it can also be easy to muck it up by making rookie mistakes. Here are some tips to help you avoid the most common mistakes.

There are thousands of loan products out there and it's a very competitive market, so it makes sense to shop around. A broker can be very useful to do the legwork. Be careful of making too many applications, though. Whenever you apply for a loan, it gets recorded in your credit file, but it doesn't say whether or not the application was approved or taken up (until after repayments have commenced). So, if you apply to a number of lenders, they will start to wonder whether you have been turned down by all the others and will get a bit nervous, and are more likely to knock you back. This is where a good broker can be worth their weight in gold. They will know what each lender can offer you and which are more likely to provide you with the right loan products and services for your individual situation.

When looking, remember that interest rates aren't everything. Sure, the interest rate is important, but there are two other considerations you need to take into account that may impact your decision as to which product to take out. First, the actual rate you pay can be seriously affected by costs such as up-front establishment fees and LMI. So, too, could the amount you will be permitted to borrow. A single person earning $85,000 with no debts or HECS liability could borrow anywhere from $596,000 to $702,924 depending on the lender. If you depend on overtime, bonuses, shift allowances or rental income to service the loan, the differences could be larger.

Second, when you take out a home loan, your lender will insist you take out building insurance. If you buy a strata title apartment, the body corporate usually handles this. Ask them for a certificate of currency. Ensure you have insurance to cover your home's contents against fire, theft or flood. If you are going to rent out your property, you should also consider landlord insurance to cover you against public liability, in case a tenant or a guest injures themselves, or a tenant damages the property. Landlord insurance can also help cover lost income if your property is damaged and can't be rented.

The most important thing is to ensure you will be able to keep paying the mortgage if you get sick or injured. This is where income protection insurance comes in: it will replace some of your income if you can't work due to sickness or injury. (See Step 4.) Mortgage protection insurance is also something you could consider getting to ensure you can always make your repayments.

Fixed or variable – or a bit of both?

Interest is what you pay to borrow someone else's money, just like you pay rent to borrow someone else's property. The interest rate is simply the amount you have to pay for each dollar you have borrowed for each year you have the money. It is usually expressed as a percentage (or cents on the dollar). A 5% interest rate means that you will have to pay five cents for every dollar you have, for each year you have it. It doesn't sound much, but it can really add up.

The rate of interest changes from time to time for a wide range of reasons. The biggest is the rate of interest the bank has to pay to get the money it is going to lend to you. The Reserve Bank cash rate – announced on the first Tuesday of every month – is a major influencer of home loan interest rates and has gone from 14.00% in August 1990 to below 1% since October 2019. Most of the time, when this rate rises, your lender will increase your rate, and when it falls, your lender will reduce your rate.

In theory, lenders can raise their interest rates whenever they wish. In practice, competition, and the ease with which you can refinance your loan, keeps them relatively honest.

When you take out a loan, you should think about how you would cope with increases in interest rates. It is always good to know that if interest rates were to rise by 2% over the next couple of years, it wouldn't put too much pressure on your monthly cash flow. If you think it might, then you should reconsider how much you propose to borrow, or consider fixing the interest rate on your loan.

You can generally choose either a fixed or variable rate, or a combination of both. But how do you know what's right for you?

Being on a variable rate can be both good and bad. When interest rates fall, your monthly payment will fall. If you choose to keep paying the same amount each month, you can repay your loan more quickly. When interest rates rise, however, you have to pay more each month; this can hurt, especially if you are on a really tight budget.

With most lenders you can choose to fix your interest rate for one to five years. A lender will base the fixed rate on their cost of funds for that period, what other lenders are doing, and their marketing strategy. Don't think of this as betting against the bank. In most cases, they will hedge their interest-rate risk by borrowing for various periods. For much of the time since 2020, the major banks have all used low fixed rates as a marketing strategy and fixed-rate borrowers have benefited. This suits the banks, because you are less likely to move to a different bank during your fixed-rate period and they can avoid passing on lower rates to their existing borrowers (a form of legal price discrimination).

Fixing your rate gives you certainty about what your monthly payments are going to be for a set period. If interest rates rise, your rate won't, so your monthly payment stays the same. The bad news is that your payment won't go down if interest rates in general go down. Fixed-rate loans tend to be less flexible in other ways, too – generally, you can't make additional payments and you can't use features such as an offset account, although a few banks have started to offer these features. A good broker will help you navigate this maze of options.

The big negative comes if you want to repay your loan before the end of the fixed-rate period – generally, you will have to pay break costs. These can be very high, especially if interest rates have fallen since you took out your fixed rate. Break costs are designed to compensate the lender for the losses incurred from letting you out of your loan. If the lender cannot resell the money at the same rate they sold it to you, then you will have to pay the difference in interest rates for the remaining period of your contract.

With most lenders, you can choose to have a combination of fixed and variable interest rates and thereby hedge your bets. Many people choose to have a bet each way by fixing a portion of their loan. This is called a 'split loan'.

Fixing all of your debt may or may not save you money. Life Sherpa's analysis of what would have happened over the past 30 years – we compared the three-year fixed rate to the average variable rate – showed that if you had fixed your rate, you would have been better off for about half the time and worse off the other half of the time. So, your choice to fix your rate or leave it variable generally comes down to a trade-off between certainty and flexibility.

Pay it off

After you've moved in and things have started to settle down, it's time to think about how you're going to pay off your home loan quickly, while at the same time achieving your other goals.

When it comes to saving or investing, it is usually best to focus on getting your home loan down at first. Then it makes sense to diversify. Why? Two reasons: risk and flexibility.

Paying off your home loan is the easiest way to get a high, risk-free, after-tax return on any spare cash you have. Paying down your home loan also creates flexibility. When your monthly payment is a low percentage of your take-home pay, you gain the flexibility to cope with reduced income, either voluntarily (such as taking time out to be with your kids, or maybe taking a sabbatical) or involuntarily (such as through redundancy or reduced hours). A low loan to value ratio also gives you flexibility to borrow more if you need it and greater bargaining power with lenders, which can get you a lower rate.

Don't fall into the trap of thinking that if some is good, more must be better. I use the guideline of getting your loan down to no less than 60% of the value of your home and the (mandatory) payments to less than 20% of your income. When you get there, it's time to think about diversifying and applying your Grow money to investment opportunities.

This means that until you get to that point, the best place for your Grow budget is in an offset account for short-term goals and as additional repayments for longer-term goals. If you think you may one day rent out your home, avoid making principal repayments – keep this money in your offset account.

Now, let's talk about how to pay off your home loan faster. Most of the following tips work on the principle of reducing the outstanding balance of your loan, on which interest is calculated daily, so you pay less interest. This means more of what you do pay goes towards reducing the outstanding balance. They involve putting as much as you can into your loan while ensuring that you can redraw some if you need to, and remembering to keep some or all or your emergency stash elsewhere.

1. **Align your mortgage payments with your payday.** This ensures your money is working for you every day, from the day you receive it, and is not sitting in another bank account for a week or more until the next mortgage payment date. So, make your payments match the frequency you get paid. If you get paid fortnightly, pay fortnightly. If you get paid monthly, pay monthly.

   Some lenders will allow you to choose the day your home loan payment is deducted. Make sure they don't just extend the first payment period. Say you get paid on the 15th of each month and you settled on the purchase of your home on 10 May. Ordinarily, the first payment would be due on 10 June. This means the money for each payment will be sitting in your transaction account for almost four weeks from when you got paid. Talk to your bank to arrange for payments to be made on the 16th of each month. But make sure the first payment is made on 16 May as a part payment, and normal payments are then made every month on the 16th.

2. **Make fortnightly payments.** If you get paid fortnightly, try paying half the normal monthly payment fortnightly. You will then in effect make an extra monthly payment each year, because there are 26 fortnights but only 12 months. If you get paid weekly, try paying a quarter of the monthly payment weekly. Don't let the bank recalculate the repayment to a weekly or fortnightly payment, though. Ask them for the monthly payment and divide by two or four as relevant.

   The normal monthly payment on a $500,000 loan at 5% is $2684. By paying $1342 fortnightly or $671 weekly, you could save four years and nine months and more than $85,000 in interest over the life of the loan. If you get paid monthly, making fortnightly payments doesn't make any sense, but you could achieve the same result by increasing the monthly payment to $2908.

3. **Use a mortgage offset account.** This can save you interest on your loan by reducing the balance on which interest is calculated. In practice, this means your mortgage account is linked to a transaction account into which your salary and other cash can be deposited and from which you withdraw money to pay expenses, bills and credit cards as these become due. For the time your money sits in this account, it is 'offset' against your loan and so reduces your interest bill. These accounts don't earn any interest on which you would have to pay tax. But make sure you are keeping enough in your offset account to justify the extra costs of a home loan with this feature. If it's less than $10,000 on average, you are likely to be better off with a no-frills loan and paying tax on the interest you earn. Your broker can help you assess this trade-off.

4. **Make additional lump-sum payments.** Use some of your tax refund or unexpected windfalls – bonuses, inheritances or lottery wins – for this.

5. **Increase your monthly payments.** Set up an extra scheduled repayment to increase your total monthly payments. Don't adjust the bank's standard payment, which will usually be processed by direct debit, but rather, set up a separate transfer so you remain in control. If you are following the Life Sherpa 50/30/20 budget, these extra payments come from your Grow bucket; don't include them in your Chore allocation with the minimum payment.

6. **If interest rates drop, don't drop your payments to match.** If you have a variable home loan and the interest rate drops, continue to pay the loan at the higher rate.

7. **Periodically review your loan to see if it is still right for you.**
   Banks are constantly offering deals to entice new borrowers that
   they don't offer to existing borrowers. However, protecting their
   so-called back book is critical to the bank's profitability. So, if you
   talk about refinancing, they will sometimes offer you the same
   deal to keep you on their books. Make sure you get a fair deal.

   It is also important to review your loan if your circumstances
   change. As your property rises in value, your income rises or
   your loan balance decreases, you may qualify for a better rate.

The third way

At the beginning of this Step, I discussed the buy-versus-rent decision
and noted that many young Australians are forging a different path by
choosing to buy their first property as an investment and rent where
they live or continue living with their parents. In fact, as many as a
third of all first-home buyers are now buying as investors. Proponents
of this arrangement, sometimes called 'rentvesting', claim that it can
provide the best of both worlds: you get to live where you want, even
if you can't afford to buy there, and you get the benefits of property
ownership. Even better, the tax system provides help along the way.
Under some circumstances, rentvesting can indeed be beneficial.
However, in my experience it's not a great strategy for most people in
the long term.

Here's what it means:

- You rent where you live (or live with your parents).
- You buy a property where you can afford to (even if this is in a
  different city).
- You get the tax benefits of negative gearing and the tenant helps
  pay your mortgage.

It is obvious why this works if you can live with your parents rent-free: the tenant pays for most of the costs of your property and the ATO chips in, so the costs of holding your property are minimal. It may seem a little less intuitive as to why it might work if you have to pay rent, but it can! As I noted earlier, the cost of owning is higher than the cost of renting (at least for the first few years). This means the price you pay to rent is less than the total of the interest, rates, maintenance and other costs of owning. Over time, this gap narrows, as rents generally rise with time – and, of course, you get the benefit of any growth in value of the property. The owner of a rental property gets a tax deduction for the shortfall, together with another tax benefit known as depreciation. This tax deduction is known as negative gearing.

Let's say there are two identical properties, one of which you own and rent out to a tenant, and the other you live in and pay rent to a landlord, paying the same rent as your tenant pays you for the property you own. The costs of ownership (interest, rates, maintenance and so on) are the same whether or not you live in the property you own, so you will only be out of pocket (before tax) by the amount you pay your property manager to manage your property and collect the rent (usually 7% of the rental income). For a property worth $650,000 and renting for $500 a week, this shortfall would amount to about $35 a week.

But after tax you will be better off. Your taxable income will be reduced by the difference between the rental income you receive and the costs of owning the property. The size of this shortfall is dependent on the interest rate you pay on your loan and how much you borrow (a higher interest rate and a bigger loan will result in a bigger shortfall), the rental yield (the ratio of rent to property value) and the depreciation benefits (newer properties will have higher deductions). The value of this tax deduction is dependent on how much you earn because that affects the rate of tax you pay.

At today's low interest rates (well below 5%) and based on a typical ten-year-old, two-bedroom apartment, the shortfall could be $15,000 or so, giving a tax benefit (for someone earning between $52,000 and $95,000 a year) of $5175, or about $100 a week. You would then be ahead (after tax) by $65 a week. The size of the benefit will reduce over time as rental income rises and the depreciation benefit falls, and will eventually disappear completely – perhaps within five to ten years.

This cash flow benefit can be valuable in helping you get through the difficult first years of ownership. But there are a few things to consider. First, most of the government benefits for first-home buyers are not available for investors. Second, CGT will be payable if you sell an investment property for more than you paid for it, and this can be significant. And keep in mind, the banks are tightening up on lending to investors, so you may need a bigger deposit and may not be able to borrow as much.

Under the right circumstances, rentvesting can give you the best of both worlds – you can afford to live where you want and you get to hedge your future housing costs. Not only that, but the Australian tax system provides a significant short-term boost to your finances. However, there are very limited circumstances in which this is a winning strategy over the long term, and so it usually provides the worst of both worlds. Capital gains tax, payable on the gain from an investment property but not on your home, will overwhelm the short-term cash flow benefits (largely from negative gearing) over time. Also, the temptation to rent a better property because of the lower initial rental price often leads people to commit a larger share of their income to housing over time. And finally, most people end up buying in a different city or region because of the lower price property available there, which means the expected hedging benefit is unlikely to be realised.

Summary

- The golden rule is to buy property, but not too much, and only when the time is right for you.
- Get into financial shape first. Check your credit report, close your unused credit cards, stop applying for credit, stay put, gather your supporting documents and get saving.
- Determine how much deposit you need. A good rule of thumb is to buy a property worth no more than five or six times your gross income.
- Determine what to buy. Make a checklist of the features that are important to you and categorise them as must-haves, nice-to-haves and would-be-goods. Consider older properties over new properties.
- Get your loan together. There are thousands of loan products out there, so shop around. Determine whether a fixed or variable rate is right for you by deciding which is a higher priority for you: certainty or flexibility.
- Pay off your home loan. Ways to do this faster include aligning your mortgage payments with your payday, making fortnightly payments, using a mortgage offset account, making additional lump-sum payments and periodically reviewing your loan to make sure it's still right for you.
- Many young Australians are 'rentvesting': renting where they live and buying an investment property elsewhere. However, there are very limited circumstances in which this is a winning strategy over the long term.

Step 8

Invest your surplus

For those of you who skipped ahead to this Step thinking it would be the exciting bit of the book, I'm about to disappoint you. Investment should be boring. If you want excitement, go to the casino or the racetrack. (This should come from the Live portion of your 50/30/20 budget, not from the Grow component!) Investment done right should not bother you day to day. If it does, you need to rethink your strategy.

Back at Step 1, I introduced the 50/30/20 rule for allocating your income. This step focuses on the third block: the Grow portion. This portion should be at least 20% of your take-home pay and is designed to support you in achieving your goals. In practice, this means it needs to do one of three things: reduce debt, provide for spending in a future period or grow income-producing assets.

While it's not my role to tell you what your goals are – that's totally up to you – I will show you how to invest this block to achieve your goals. But you have to have your financial house in order; that is, you must have a regular income, spend less than you earn every pay day, have gotten rid of your red debts and have an emergency stash of at least three months' spending. Until you can tick all of these boxes, your Grow allocation should go to debt reduction or building an emergency stash. If you haven't yet bought your home, you might think of allocating it to saving a home deposit, in which case this chapter will help you work out where you should keep it in the meantime.

Pay down your mortgage, invest or contribute to super?

If you're a homeowner with a mortgage and you've got some spare cash, should you pay down your mortgage, invest or make additional super contributions? The right answer boils down to a trade-off between lifetime return, certainty and flexibility. So, the answer is, 'It depends'.

To help you decide, I'll use three examples of people each with a $400,000 home loan at an interest rate of 2.5% who have $10,000 saved and can commit to saving $500 a month. (I have assumed that all of them earn between $51,000 and $120,000 a year and so pay tax at 32.5% plus the Medicare levy of 2%.) Let's compare the outcome for these three people over ten years:

1. Kate uses the savings to make an immediate principal repayment of $10,000 and additional monthly repayments of $500 on her home loan.
2. Chris invests the $10,000 in a portfolio of a wide range of shares and bonds and makes additional investments in the same portfolio every month.
3. Sarah makes a tax-deductible contribution of $10,000 to her super and then makes monthly salary sacrifice contributions which reduce her take-home pay by $500 a month.

Let's take a look at the outcomes.

The first scenario, making extra mortgage repayments, is the simplest to set up. All you have to do is deposit the cash into your home loan account. Kate makes an immediate payment of $10,000, reducing her home loan straight away by $10,000 to $390,000. This saves her interest every month so that more of her regular payment goes to paying off principal, allowing her to pay off her loan faster. She then sets up an automated payment of an additional $500 each month.

Over ten years she puts aside $60,000 ($500 multiplied by 120 months) plus the initial $10,000 for a total of $70,000. At the end of ten years, she has reduced her home loan balance by $80,293. In effect, she has earned the mortgage rate (2.5%) after tax to make a total return of $10,293. The result would be the same whether she made additional repayments or deposited the money in her offset account.

This strategy delivers a risk-free return, is simple to set up and can be stopped at any time, and you can usually access your savings by redrawing the funds or refinancing your home loan. However, in a low-interest-rate environment, the return is correspondingly low.

In the next scenario, Chris takes his savings and invests in an investment portfolio. In this case, I have used the Vanguard High Growth Index Fund, not because I particularly recommend it, but because it invests in a broad range of assets and I have 18 years of historical data to look back on. This period includes both the GFC (2008) and the COVID-19 period (2020, in case you've been living under a rock), and so spans a good mixture of good and bad times.

Over the 18 years since its inception (at the time of writing), this fund has delivered an average annual return (after fees, before taxes) of 8.42%, comprising 5.3% income distributed each year and 3.11% capital growth. The split matters because the annual income return is taxed at your ordinary tax rate when received, whereas you only pay tax on the capital return when you sell and will usually get the CGT discount, meaning you only pay tax on half the gain. In this example I have assumed that Chris pays the tax on the distribution each year and reinvests the after-tax amount.

After ten years, Chris sells the whole investment, pays tax on the gain and nets $100,367 for a return of $30,367 on his $70,000 investment. Of course, past performance is no guarantee of future performance, so there is some degree of uncertainty about the return, which may turn out to be higher or lower in practice. Importantly, as markets fluctuate, you may not be able to realise the amount you expect if you need the money in a hurry before the end of the ten years.

The higher return comes at the expense of less certainty and some flexibility. It also takes a little more work to set it up in the first place. Take professional advice before embarking on this strategy. Google is no substitute for quality advice when choosing an investment vehicle to implement this strategy.

In the final scenario, Sarah uses her savings to make tax-deductible super contributions with both the initial $10,000 and the ongoing $500 monthly savings. For simplicity and ease of comparison, I have assumed that Sarah invests in the same assets as Chris did in the second scenario, but through a super fund. This works because you get a tax deduction for contributing extra to your super and your super fund pays just 15% tax on the money it receives. Moreover, any super fund pays tax at 15% on income and an effective 10% on capital gains (15% on two-thirds of the growth).

As a result, the initial $10,000 savings will result in a net investment of $11,433 ($10,000 plus the tax deduction of $3,450 less contributions tax of $2,017), which gives compound interest a larger base to start working from. Similarly, to take home $500, you need to earn $763, so by salary-sacrificing $763 each month, Sarah reduces her take-home pay by $500 (the amount she is happy to save) but $649 ends up in her super fund.

After ten years, Sarah's $70,000 in savings has turned into $137,293. The good news is that when she turns 60, she could receive this money tax-free. The bad news is that she can't access it until she turns 60.

The third scenario – investing in super – delivers the highest lifetime return based on the tax advantages. However, these advantages come with restrictions on access. For many younger people, this lack of flexibility is a deal-breaker. If you think you might need the money before you turn 60 – for example, if you are planning early retirement, or you are setting aside money to pay for your kids' school fees or start a business – this strategy will be unsuitable.

I would usually only recommend this approach if you have already built up a pool of investments outside super and have your home loan at a manageable level, or you are close to age 60. It is particularly important to accumulate sufficient assets outside super to achieve your pre-retirement goals and provide for contingencies such as losing your job and not being able to find another. A 2015 study of 50- to 75-year-olds by the Financial Services Council and Commonwealth Bank showed that of those who had retired, 23% did so because of ill health and 14% because of redundancy. So, until you have accumulated sufficient assets, keep saving and investing outside super.

The second scenario – invest outside super – delivers a higher return than paying off your home loan without giving up access to the money. I would recommend this as the preferred strategy for people who might need the money before age 60 but are looking at a medium to long timeframe (five or more years), and who have their home loan at a manageable level.

The first scenario delivers the lowest return but with great certainty, and is the preferred option if you need access to the money in the short term or you have a relatively large home loan. So, how do you decide when your home loan is manageable and it's time to move on to the second strategy? It all depends on your circumstances and attitude to risk. I suggest you use two measures when assessing this:

1. **Your LVR.** Is your LVR more than 80%? If so, focus on paying down your home loan. An LVR below 80% will allow you to avoid LMI if you want to refinance and will enable you to take advantage of getting a lower interest rate. How much less than 80% should you aim for? It depends on your attitude to risk and what might happen to your income in future. For example, are you and your partner planning to have a family and drop to one salary? For many, 70% is a suitable threshold to consider.

2. **Your payments relative to your income.** If your mandatory monthly home loan payment is less than 20% of your take-home income, it's probably time to start diverting savings somewhere else. For example, if you make $70,000 a year, your monthly take-home pay (assuming no HECS) will be $4615, so if your loan repayments are less than $923, it's time to think about an alternative strategy.

Ready to invest?

If you've decided paying off your home loan is for you, go back and read Step 7. If you've concluded that more super is best for you, go back and read Step 5. If you still can't decide, talk to an adviser. But if you've concluded that investing is for you, then read on.

Start with the goal in mind and the date you want to achieve it. You now have two variables to manage: how much of your Grow portion you are prepared or able to allocate to achieving this goal, and the return you need to generate on the money you have set aside. The further away your deadline is, the more important the return element is. In fact, as much as two-thirds of what you will spend in retirement comes from these earnings, so fees and returns are critically important.

For short-term goals, though, it is mostly about the amount you set aside, as returns will play only a small part. The higher the return you need to achieve, the higher the risk you will have to be prepared to take (I'll explain what I mean by risk shortly). The level of risk will also affect the level of confidence you can have about the precise date you will achieve your goal.

Your personality is also important. If you are going to panic or get depressed or anxious when you see the value of your savings decline due to market movements, then you may have to learn how to deal with this or be prepared to set aside more money for your goals.

- **For short-term goals** – goals with a target date less than three years away, such as a gap year, a new car or other major purchase, or the deposit on your new home – focus on certainty. With such a short period for your money to get to work, the outcome will be driven primarily by the cash you set aside. You should focus on predictable investment outcomes, access when you need it, and safety, even at the expense of returns. If you qualify, consider using the First Home Super Saver Scheme. Otherwise, bank deposits will be the most common solution. If you already have a home loan, an offset account is likely to give the best outcome. Shares and property are generally unsuitable. Expect a return of 1% (before tax) or so on deposits and up to 3% (after tax) on an offset account.
- **For medium-term goals** – goals with a target date at least three years away but less than seven years or so – focus on trying to improve returns a little by including some growth assets (which I'll explain in more detail later, but for now think shares). The period is not really long enough for property due to the high

transaction costs of buying and selling. As your goal gets closer, start to lock in gains by moving to bank deposits or your offset account. Expect a return of 5% (before tax) or so on a mixture of shares and deposits and up to 3% (after tax) on an offset account.

- **For long-term goals** – goals with a target date between, say, 7 and 15 years, such as providing for your children's education – focus more on achieving better returns by including more growth assets, including shares and property. Look to gradually invest, rather than buying all at one time. If you pay a high rate of tax (earning over $120,000, where the rate jumps to 39% including Medicare), look at managing tax by using tax-effective products such as insurance bonds, or investing in the name of a lower earning partner. Expect a return of 6% to 7% (before tax) or so on a mixture of shares, property and deposits, and up to 3% (after tax) on an offset account.

- **For very long-term goals** – goals with a target date exceeding 15 years, especially retirement saving – focus mostly on growth assets, including shares and property. Pay particular attention to fees and tax, and for retirement savings, take advantage of the tax savings provided by super. Cash and bank deposits are generally unsuitable. Aim for a return of inflation plus 4% to 5%, or about 6.5% to 8% after tax in super.

Understanding risk

Risk is all around us. Identifying it, understanding it and managing it is key to a safe, secure and sufficiently interesting life. But when it comes to investing, fear of risk can lead to indecision. To succeed, we need to embrace risk and understand the balance between sleeping easily at night and generating the desired rate of return. By embracing risk, I don't mean heading to the casino and putting it all on black.

I mean understanding it and aligning your goals, personality and investments to achieve the best possible outcome.

The higher the risk you take, the higher the return you should expect to generate. Note that I didn't say high risk leads to high returns. Most problems arise when the expected return doesn't reflect the risk, or the level of risk doesn't match the investor's goals. But what is risk? And what does it mean for your money?

Most people think of risk in the context of losing their money. Professional investors usually talk about risk as variability of returns or the likelihood they will get a return that is different to the average of the market they are investing in. I take a much broader view, a view that is much more relevant to individuals. I think of risk as the probability of whatever plan you choose delivering the outcome you expect, over the period you have, with the amount you choose to set aside. A high-risk strategy will have a low likelihood of delivering the outcome you desire, whereas a low-risk strategy will have a high likelihood of giving you what you set out to achieve. There are no absolute certainties in this game. You should be seeking clarity and confidence instead.

Whether you are saving a deposit for your first home or putting aside money for retirement, most financial goals require one or more contributions of money, selection of a product or strategy and a period of time in which to achieve the outcome.

Don't stress about day-to-day movements

Every day you can see reports of the activity on the financial markets – share prices went up ('rallied' or 'firmed') or down ('fell', 'eased' or 'plummeted'); bond yields eased (the price went up) or rallied (the price went down). Similarly, hundreds of websites, newspapers and other publications cover these gyrations, desperately seeking to find reasons for apparently random movements. This is mostly noise and should, for the most part, be ignored. Once it is in the paper or on TV, it is too late to take advantage of it.

In fact, paying too much attention to market noise and checking the value of your investment can be counterproductive and simply add stress to your life. What's worse, it may even be bad for your wealth.

In his book, *Fooled by Randomness: The Hidden Role of Chance in Life and in the Markets*, Nassim Nicholas Taleb makes the point that according to the prospect theory – developed by Daniel Kahneman and Amos Tversky to help explain decision making under uncertainty – 'for every good result you see, you gain one Emotional Unit … a loss has twice the impact on your emotions, [so] for a bad result you lose two Emotional Units'. This means that on days when you check and the market is up, you feel good and a tad richer. But on days when the market is down, you start to worry and you feel less rich. This feeling can lead to panic decisions, which can cost you money. The more often you check, the more stress you feel. Emotions and how you deal with them are a key influence on investor success.

Not only do losses upset us by a greater margin than the joy of gains, but the more you look, the more likely you are to observe a down day. Let me explain with some statistics. You don't need to worry too much about how I got the numbers, but they are typical of how this would play out for an investor over a 20-year period (for a typical portfolio with a volatility of 10%). If this investor checks their portfolio value daily, they will have a 54% chance of seeing a gain on any given day. Over the 20 years, they will see a gain on 2700 days and a loss on 2300 days, giving them a gain of 2700 emotional units while losing 4600 emotional units.

If the investor only checks monthly, the odds of an up day improve to 67%. In this case, they will gain 161 emotional units, while losing 158 emotional units. Their emotions start to look more in balance, and they feel better. Check quarterly and, miraculously, there is a 77% chance of seeing a gain on any given occasion. Now the investor sees

62 up days and only 18 down days, leading to a positive emotional unit balance heading towards two to one (a gain of 62 and a loss of 36). And while I don't recommend this approach, if the investor could resist looking for a whole year, they would have a 93% of seeing a gain, and would be up by 19 emotional units and down just 2 units.

This is why linking your super account (or your home loan for that matter) to your internet banking is a really bad idea – the balance in your super fund is displayed when you log in to your bank account. I'm sure people in IT at the various banks thought this was a great idea, but it is simply bad for your stress levels. Don't do it!

I'm not suggesting that when it comes to your investments you should simply set and forget, but too much checking can lead to emotional stress and cause you to make unwise moves trying to avoid a temporary loss or capture the next big thing.

Periodic rebalancing of your investments will also help. Over time, differences in the performance of the components of your portfolio will result in their relative proportions moving away from your initial plan. When you rebalance, you sell some of the investments that have gone up and buy more of those that have gone down, restoring the balance.

Asset allocation

Assets are things you can invest in, and there are really only two types: defensive and growth.

Defensive assets have lower, more stable returns. They include cash, bank deposits and bonds. Most of the return comes as income; that is, the value of the asset doesn't generally change much, but it creates an income stream, usually called interest. These assets are suited to short-term goals or helping smooth returns for long-term goals. They are generally incapable of beating inflation over longer periods.

Growth assets have higher expected returns that vary from year to year. They include shares, property and infrastructure. They are suited to achieving longer-term goals, as they have the capacity to grow faster than inflation. Generally, they will create some income from dividends or rent, and much of the overall return comes from growth in the value of the asset.

How you allocate your investments between defensive and growth is called 'asset allocation', and it is the biggest determinant of returns. It will contribute more than 70% of the return. This means how much you allocate to shares compared to bonds or property is far more important than which share or property you choose. Get this bit right and the rest will ordinarily follow.

Factors suggesting a higher allocation to growth assets include a longer timeframe, your ability to recover from material capital losses, your ability to give the market time to recover from paper losses and your likelihood of panic-selling in the face of paper losses. The opposite factors – a shorter timeframe, material loss of capital having dire consequences, a lack of time to allow the market to recover from paper losses and a high likelihood of panic reactions to paper losses – suggest a higher allocation to defensive assets.

Traditionally, financial planners have used risk-profiling tools to assess the appropriate investments for their clients. This approach isn't always successful, however, because it ignores other aspects of personality that are just as important. It asks clients abstract questions they are ill-equipped to answer, and the language used can lead them to the wrong conclusion.

For example, this approach seeks to classify people into groups usually described as 'conservative', 'balanced', 'assertive' or 'aggressive', based on their knowledge and risk tolerance. I am yet to meet a client who would describe themselves as 'aggressive' when it comes to investing, regardless of how much they are actually comfortable with. Most people will instinctively think, 'These are my retirement savings; I have to be careful with them'. If you are in your 20s or 30s, this is possibly the worst position you could take when it comes to retirement savings, as it will almost guarantee you won't have enough when it comes time to retire. This approach tends to lead investors to under-allocate towards defensive assets for medium-term goals and to over-allocate towards defensive assets for retirement savings. In both cases, this often leads to a greater likelihood of missing the target.

By focusing on broader personality traits such as confidence, involvement and anxiety, and on your life goals and timeframes, you can get to a better asset allocation decision.

'Strategy' is how you choose to invest in assets (such as via direct purchase, managed funds or super), and the way you manage the assets and the tax consequences. For example, you could invest in defensive assets by going to your bank and depositing money in a term deposit or high-interest online account. You could go to a fund manager and invest in a cash management trust or bond fund, or you could buy an exchange traded fund (ETF) through a stockbroker or online. You could also use your super fund. All of these options invest in broadly the same underlying asset but will have different fees associated with buying and selling as well as managing your money. They may also give different after-tax returns.

Here is my five-step process for choosing your strategy:

1. Select your asset allocation to match your goal (X% growth/ Y% defensive).
2. Choose asset classes within this allocation (shares, property, bonds or cash).
3. Decide how the investment is to be funded (cash, super money or borrowing).
4. Decide who is to own it (self, partner, jointly, family trust or self-managed super fund).

5. Choose the investment vehicle (direct purchase, managed fund, listed investment company, ETF, insurance bond or super fund).

If you are already a homeowner, step three (how you fund the investment) can make a material difference to your after-tax return, so it's important to consider debt recycling (more on this later) before you transfer money to your investment account.

Now, let's look at the two most common types of growth assets – shares and property – in a bit more detail.

Shares, ETFs, bonds and managed funds

Shares represent a portion of the ownership in a particular business. The company uses the money to fund its business and the owners of the shares receive a return from the profits of the business, called a dividend. If the underlying business makes a profit and pays tax, the dividend will come with a credit for tax paid by the company. This is called a franking credit and can significantly improve the returns to an investor.

Listed shares, the ones you are likely to invest in, trade on a stock exchange. This means you can buy or sell by placing an order through a stockbroker. These days, this is mostly done online. The price you pay or receive is driven by the consensus of all the buyers and sellers at the time. If more people want to buy than there are sellers, the price will move up. If more want to sell than buy, the price will fall.

The total value of the 2200 shares listed on the Australian Securities Exchange (ASX) is $2.6 trillion, and each day about $6.5 billion changes hands. This turnover means the market is liquid at least for the 300 largest companies, so you can get in and out when you want for as little as $5 in brokerage, and the prices are transparent.

There is a widespread perception that investing on the stock market is little more than gambling. Certainly, this is true for some. Day traders buy and sell quickly, sometimes on little more than a hunch or because everyone else is doing it. Sometimes they make money; sometimes they don't. In contrast, a long-term hold of a portfolio of quality companies is a good way to get rich slowly.

A range of shares is important, as this provides protection from company-specific issues. It is best to spread your investment among a few big companies (large-cap shares) and smaller companies (small or mid caps), and across industries (such as financials, resources, industrials, infrastructure and property). It is also a good idea to include some shares from overseas companies from various countries. After all, Australia represents less than 2% of the value of all shares listed on all the stock exchanges around the world. The Australian market is also dominated by financial and resource companies and offers little opportunity to invest in technology companies, for example.

If you have limited funds, it can be difficult to spread your funds over enough different shares. The minimum parcel of a share you can buy is $500. Brokerage is usually fixed for small parcels and will usually cost from $5.

If you were to buy a parcel of ASX 200 shares (broadly the 200 largest companies on the exchange), starting with the minimum of the smallest and buying everything else in proportion to the value of the exchange that they represent (market-capitalisation weighted), you would need $1.5 million. This is why many smaller investors use managed funds (some of which trade on the stock exchange and are therefore known as exchange traded funds, or ETFs) to invest in potentially hundreds of companies with a single trade.

Bonds, on the other hand, are loans to companies, governments or other entities. They pay regular interest and will return the face value at maturity. This is why they are often referred to as 'fixed-income' investments. Interest can be at a fixed rate or a variable rate tied to a benchmark. When interest rates rise, the value of fixed-rate bonds will fall. Conversely, when rates fall, the value of fixed-rate bonds will rise. Despite these day-to-day changes to the price at which you can buy or sell a bond, you will only get back the face value at maturity. This means your investment is not capable of growing over time, and that's why they are defensive assets.

It can be difficult for small investors to buy bonds directly, because they trade in larger parcels. A small number of bonds are now listed on the ASX, however, and more are expected to join them. In the meantime, most people choose to invest in bonds through managed funds or ETFs.

The other defensive asset used by most investors is gold. Ray Dalio – Chief Investment Officer at Bridgewater Associates, the world's largest hedge fund – believes that everyone should have some gold in their portfolio. He says, 'There is no sensible reason [not to own gold] other than you don't know history or you don't know the economics of it'. I agree and have always held some gold in my investments. Gold has an impressive track record of holding its value or rising when other assets fall, adding diversification to portfolios and reducing volatility, which can deliver better risk-adjusted returns. Its legacy of diversification and low correlation with many other traditional asset classes has made it a 'safe-haven' asset during times of market turbulence.

Active versus index

When you choose to invest in shares, it is possible that you might choose a few shares from the more than 2200 ASX listings, or one of thousands of bonds issued by companies and governments. Unless you have a larger sum to invest, it is more likely that you will do so by investing in a fund. This enables you to spread the risk by investing in a larger basket of shares and perhaps benefit from the skill of a professional manager. If you are investing in bonds, it is even more likely that you will invest through a fund, because of the difficulty of buying small parcels of bonds and the fact that many bonds are available to professional investors only. But are you getting value for the fees you pay to a fund?

The best way to assess fund managers is to check how they compare to each other and to the overall market in which they're investing. The most common measure of how the market as a whole performs is an index. For example, in Australia, the All Ordinaries (All Ords) and the S&P/ASX 200 are the most popular indexes. You will usually hear them being reported on the news each day.

The All Ords measures the performance of the top 500 companies, whereas the S&P/ASX 200 is limited to the top 200. They do this by looking at the value of a portfolio consisting of the relevant companies in proportion to the total value of their shares. Periodically, they add or remove companies to account for new companies being listed, and others being merged, taken over or going out of business. There are other indexes that track the performance of segments of the market, such as property funds, financial companies or industrial companies.

There is a growing group of funds that invest in all of the companies in a particular index. These are called indexed funds because the manager doesn't seek to pick winners. This means they are cheap, with the typical fund costing between 0.05% and 0.30% of assets under management. Often these funds are referred to as 'passive funds', but I don't like the use of 'passive' in this context. The choice of an index is very much an active decision and will drive more of your returns than the fund manager you choose to replicate it. I prefer to use 'indexed' as it more clearly describes what's going on.

You can invest in these by buying units in a managed fund direct from the manager (usually through a financial planner or platform). Alternatively, you can buy shares in an ETF listed on the stock exchange using a stockbroker, including online brokers such as Opentrader, Pearler, SelfWealth or CommSec. It's mostly a personal preference, but managed funds can be cheaper (because you don't have to pay brokerage) if you are buying small parcels or want to set up a regular investment plan. ETFs can be cheaper if you are buying larger parcels. When the total size of the fund is shrinking, ETFs can be more tax-efficient; but this last point is a bit esoteric, and why would you choose to invest in a fund that was shrinking over time anyway?

Managed funds and their listed equivalent (listed investment companies), which seek to add value by picking which shares to buy, tend to have higher fees and, because they turn over their holdings, can trigger greater tax for investors. Therefore, an active fund manager has to be able to do better by making more investment earnings than their fees and the extra tax impost in order for investors to come out ahead. Do they? This is a pretty controversial question. As a group, it is mathematically impossible for them all to outperform (I'll explain why in a moment). But clearly some do. Very few do so for lengthy periods. The trick is picking which one will.

To understand why, you need to understand that the share market and the bond market are zero-sum games. For every investor that outperforms, there must be one that underperforms. So, the aggregate of the outperformances must be less than the aggregate of the underperformances when you deduct fees and taxes. It is possible that the underperformers are the small mug punters without the benefit of the professional researchers. Unfortunately, professional and institutional investors own about 73% of the shares on the ASX. Although this may provide a small pool of outperformance, it is unlikely to be sufficient.

S&P Dow Jones Indices, a company that creates and manages indexes around the world, tracks this data and publishes a regular score card called the 'SPIVA®'. Although it has a vested interest in spruiking its indexes, the data is clear: almost three-quarters of Australian big company managers, and almost four-fifths of international share managers, fail to beat their index over five years. Similar results are seen in other markets and countries.

The areas where significant numbers of managers do add value are small companies, emerging markets and specific industry sectors. This is probably due to the fact that there is less research performed on those companies, which creates greater opportunities for those who do the research. Australia does not have a tradable index that tracks stocks outside the top 300 (S&P/ASX 300). The so-called Small Ordinaries tracks only companies ranked from 101 to 300. Therefore, in order to benefit from active management, you need to be able to identify the small proportion of managers who can outperform after accounting for the additional fees. Is it possible to do this consistently?

SPIVA researchers and their colleagues at Morningstar also track top-performing Australian share funds over longer periods and few maintain their outperformance over longer periods. Even professional investors have a poor track record of picking managers that outperform. Research by Amit Goyal and Sunil Wahal examined 8755 manager selections by 3700 pension fund managers over a 10-year period. The ones they hired outperformed in the three years before being hired (by 2.9%) and underperformed (by 0.5%) in the three years after being hired. On the other hand, the ones they fired underperformed before being fired (by 1.3%) and outperformed after being fired (by 0.8%). So, if the professionals can't do it, what makes you think you can?

This is why the regulator makes fund managers include the disclaimer that past performance is not a reliable indicator of future performance in advertisements. The problem is not that fund managers are incompetent; it's just that it is a really tough trick to pull off, especially when costs and taxes are considered. And it gets harder the larger your fund becomes. More importantly, the incentives aren't there.

You see, in order to obtain a different result, you have to do something different. This means you have to invest in a group of stocks that differs materially from the index. Sometimes this will be different good and sometimes it will be different bad. Few investors have the stomach to tolerate long periods of different bad in order to enjoy the benefits of different good. This is bad for business if you are running a funds management business and bad for your career if you are a fund manager, so most avoid it and become closet index investors. A good indicator that a manager is doing this is to listen to how they describe their approach. If they use words like 'overweight' or 'underweight', they are likely to be guilty here. Also look at their top ten holdings – is it different to the index's top ten constituents?

The research on investment managers shows that the best indicators of a high-performing fund manager are low fees, a high active share and high levels of manager ownership in the fund. Funds with lower expense ratios tended to outpace indexes more often. This makes sense, because it gives them a lower bar to clear to beat indexes. Funds whose managers had invested more dollars into their funds also tended to outpace more often, probably because their interests are more closely aligned with investors'. These two factors tend to align with other traits that could also add value: lower portfolio turnover (which reduces transaction costs) and lower staff turnover.

Whatever the data shows, it is clear that identifying high-performing managers is an intensive and time-consuming task, which will add another layer of costs and result in greater transaction costs as money is moved from fund to fund. I firmly believe that for small investors with less than $1 million to invest, it is unlikely that the extra cost of this analysis will be consistently rewarded for large-company and international shares. However, it can be rewarding for small-company share funds.

Investors generally do worse than the funds they invest in. You might have to read that sentence again, as it sounds quite strange. Investors tend to invest based on past returns, and so tend to invest in funds after they have done well. As I noted previously, the top funds this year tend not to be the top funds next year. This means that investors are more likely to buy when a fund is about to underperform and to not invest in funds when they are new and therefore more likely to outperform. As a result, investors will do worse, on average, than the overall performance of the fund.

This behaviour is one of the biggest negative impacts on investor return. In fact, research by Vanguard suggests that the reason investors who use a financial adviser do better than those who don't is not that the adviser is necessarily better at picking funds, but that the adviser moderates the investor's behaviour. Vanguard says this factor can explain two-thirds or more of the increased performance.

Property investment

Investing in bricks and mortar is ingrained in the Australian psyche, and it has played an important role in wealth creation for generations. In fact, it is difficult to imagine a lifetime investment plan that does not incorporate some real estate. However, this is not to say that it is a guaranteed way to get rich, and it shouldn't be the only way. The key is to not get too carried away with all the hype.

You will hear lots of talk about various property investment strategies: houses or units, negative or positive cash flow property, negative gearing or hotspotting. There are also more advanced strategies, such as renovating for profit, flipping off-the-plan, property development and land banking. I am sure you can find people who claim to have made a fortune using these strategies, but they are high risk and not for the faint-hearted. I don't believe they are appropriate for people without specific skills and the time and interest to commit to them. I suggest you focus more on the get-rich-slowly approach: buy good-quality property in the right location, look after it and hold it for a long time.

Sounds easy? As you can guess, there is more to it than meets the eye. And the decision process is quite different to how you choose your home – don't confuse the two. Here are a few ground rules that will help:

- Buy property around the median price for the suburb.
- Focus on the attraction of the property for tenants – they are going to pay your bills and make you money.
- Buy property that is typical of the suburb: if you are going to buy in a suburb renowned for its Victorian terraces, don't buy a brand-new apartment. If it is a suburb that attracts families, buy a house or larger unit.
- Avoid high-density blocks: stick to low-rise, boutique blocks or houses.
- Avoid new or off-the-plan properties, especially house and land packages on the fringes of cities.
- Buy close to amenities that the type of tenant would want, such as transport, cafes or schools.
- Know your plan B: can you hold on if your property is vacant for a few weeks, or a few months? You don't want to be a forced seller.
- Get the right insurance.
- Make sure your loan is structured right – consider an interest-only mortgage, beware of cross-collateralising (using more than one property as security for a mortgage) and learn the lessons of debt recycling (see page 191). Don't do this without a good mortgage broker.
- Do your research. Be wary of information provided by agents or others who will receive a commission if you buy.

Your own suburb or nearby may not be the best place to buy at the time you are ready to buy. It will leave your wealth very concentrated, but it does mean your information advantage can help you get a better deal, and you are close by to keep an eye on it. If you are going to buy elsewhere, think about how you can do the research. You might need the help of a buyer's agent.

Use a good agent to manage your property. Don't try to become an expert in tenancy law. Having a third party between you and your tenant can make it easier to put up the rent and to limit maintenance to the essentials.

Positive cash flow or negative gearing?

You'll hear arguments all the time about whether it's better to be negatively geared or to try to find a property with positive cash flow. It hinges on whether you will make a profit each year or need to contribute to the cost of holding the property. It's a nonsense argument. For a start, it confuses the property purchase decision with the funding decision. By this I mean that whether or not the property is a good investment is an entirely different decision to how you should pay for it.

All tenanted property is cash flow–positive to a degree, in the sense that the rental income will exceed the cost of maintenance, agent's fees and rates. This surplus may or may not be enough to fund your interest bill, depending on how much you borrow.

As you will learn later in the chapter, if you have a home loan you should aim to recycle your debt – so, the funds you've saved to buy the investment property should be repaid off your home loan and a redraw used to fund the purchase. This funding choice doesn't affect the quality of the property investment, and it will create a negative gearing position for your tax return because the total deductions for interest, depreciation, maintenance, agent's fees and rates will exceed the income. This creates a tax benefit.

Time is your biggest asset. Over the long term, property will generally rise in line with household incomes. As I explained earlier, Australian households have spent broadly the same proportion of their incomes on housing for a very long time, so as incomes rise, the amount people can dedicate to housing will rise. Together with interest rates and bank lending policies, this drives the amount people can pay for property. Rising interest rates or tightening lending policies would see the price people are prepared to pay for property rise less quickly, or even fall. Whatever short-term fluctuations this may cause, the longer you can hold on, the greater the likelihood that you will see capital growth.

Shares or property?

The debate as to whether you should invest in shares or (residential) property rages at barbeques across the nation, in online investor forums and in the media. The property camp argue that it is difficult to lose your entire investment in property, it's easier to borrow to buy property, it's easier to understand – after all, everyone's a property expert if they've bought their own home! – and you can see and touch it. The shares camp argues that it's easier to diversify because you can buy smaller parcels, the income is higher and comes with franking credits, and it is easier to get in and out without the stamp duty, agent's fees and other costs of property.

This is a nonsense argument. Over most long periods, both have performed similarly. The ASX and Russell Investments regularly prepare a long-term investing report, which compares various investment options over long periods. The 2018 report shows that over 20 years, a top-rate taxpayer (earning over $180,000) would have earned, after tax, 9.1% in residential property and 8.0% on Australian shares, with both investments funded with 50% debt. A taxpayer on the lowest rate (earning less than $45,000) would have earned 10.4% in property and 9.7% in shares.

The real question should not be shares or property, but rather how much of each. A balanced investment portfolio should contain some of each. This provides diversification and helps smooth out returns.

And don't confuse residential property investing with the real estate portion of your share investing! These two things behave entirely differently and are not substitutes. Companies such as Goodman Group (GMG), Mirvac (MGR), Dexus (DXS), and Stockland (SGP) make up 7% of the ASX 200. These companies invest in offices, factories, shopping centres, warehouses and property development, and form an important element in your share investing.

Debt recycling

Debt reycling isn't quite like recycling your newspapers or bottles, but much as that is good for the environment, this is good for your wallet. Debt recycling is the process of turning non-deductible debt into deductible debt. It works to save you money because the interest paid on debt used to fund an investment is tax deductible, whereas interest paid on your home loan is not.

In practice, this means that if you have $10,000 to invest, you could use it to, say, buy some shares. Alternatively, you could use it to repay some of the outstanding balance on your home loan, then redraw $10,000 on your home loan and use that money to invest in the same shares. Nothing has really changed: you still owe the same amount on your home loan, and you still have the same $10,000 of shares. But now the interest on the $10,000 is tax deductible.

Here's how the numbers look. Suzie has a salary of $90,000. She pays tax of $21,517, leaving an after-tax income of $68,483. She has a home loan balance of $400,000 at 2.89% interest, so she pays $11,560 in interest in a year. She has saved $10,000 to invest in shares, on which she expects to earn $500 (although the actual return has no impact on the benefit of investing with or without debt recycling).

In scenario A, she uses the $10,000 to buy the shares. In scenario B, she uses the $10,000 to reduce her home loan to $390,000 and then redraws $10,000, which she uses to invest. Her personal balance sheet is no different. But when you look at Suzie's income, things change for the better. The benefit of $184 after tax is the equivalent of earning an extra 1.84% on the investment after tax. The higher your tax rate, the bigger the benefit.

This means that if you are investing and still have money owing on your home loan, you will usually be better off if you use the funds to pay down your home loan and invest using funds redrawn from your home loan.

To decide if this is for you, ask yourself the following questions: Do you have a home loan on your home (not an investment property), and have you saved up some cash? Is the balance outstanding on your home loan less than 80% of the valuation of your home? Do you want to invest or pay down the home loan? If you decide to invest, then consider debt recycling.

Make sure you set this system up properly. Interest is only tax deductible if it is being paid on a loan used to acquire an investment or to refinance a loan previously used to acquire an investment. It is vital that the flow of funds from the draw-down on the loan to the purchase or refinance is clear and the funds do not get mixed in with funds on which the interest is not deductible. This means the borrowed funds should never be placed in an offset account prior to being invested. It also means that you should have a separate loan account (or split) for the investment portion. Now might be a great time to review your home loan to make sure it's right for you and your debt recycling activities.

Once you're properly set up, follow these steps:

1. Take the $10,000 you have saved and make a repayment on your home loan.
2. Ask your lender to create a separate split for the undrawn portion of your limit (now increased by $10,000). Most banks will allow you to split your loan into as many separate facilities as you need.
3. Draw the $10,000 and transfer it directly to the cash account associated with your share trading account.
4. Never deposit other monies into this split in your home loan.
5. If you can, make the split interest-only to maximise the benefit – although be careful of paying a higher interest rate for this feature. Your financial planner or accountant will help you assess if the tax benefit exceeds the cost.
6. Enjoy the benefit!

A good broker will help you set this up for worry-free debt recycling.

Starting small

If you are starting your investment portfolio with a small amount – anything less than $500 a month or $10,000 as lump sum – use this more as an opportunity to learn about yourself. The most valuable lesson you can learn at this stage is how you react when your investments go up or down. If they go up, do you think you're the next Warren Buffett? Or do you just get a warm feeling inside? If they go down, do you feel like selling and hiding under the doona? Or do you feel like buying more? These insights into your reactions to volatility will stand you in good stead when you're ready to get serious.

With a small sum, the best place to get this experience is one of the micro-investing platforms such as Raiz or Spaceship. With a little more (say, $1000 a month or a lump sum of more than $10,000), consider one of the low-cost share-trading sites such as Opentrader, Pearler or SelfWealth.

Raiz and Spaceship both offer diversified investments with a range of risk and return profiles. Don't get too obsessed with returns, fees or structure at this point. The important thing is to get started, gather a pool of investments large enough to get serious and learn some valuable personal lessons. Personally, I'm a big fan of Raiz, mostly because it is more diversified and the rewards and round-up features will quickly add to your stash.

The most significant impact you can have on growing your investment at this stage is how much you invest, so have a plan to add some more. If you automate this, it will make it easier and avoid you having to decide what day to invest. Raiz makes this easy with their cool round-up feature.

If you've got more than $20,000 (or $10,000 and can commit to $500 a month), you're ready to get serious, and some professional advice before investing will pay long-term dividends – pun intended!

At this point, set a goal. Work out why you are investing. Maybe you are saving to buy your first home or investment property, or perhaps to pay for your kids' school fees. In most cases, you will have an amount in mind and a date when you'll need it. There are only three levers you can pull to achieve your goal: the amount you invest, how long you invest for and the return you earn (net of fees). You can generally only choose two of these, and they will determine what the third needs to be. Not all combinations are possible.

At this stage, again, how much you invest will have the largest impact, and your goal will help you stick to the plan. If you need help setting a goal, go back and read 'Setting goals' on page 24). The secret to success here is to get invested, stay invested (being aware of your behaviour and biases) and invest some more – don't let temporary market declines or spending impulses distract you or derail your plan.

Don't obsess too much about fees at this point. Some fees are fixed amounts (such as account fees) and so can work out to be a large percentage of your potential returns. For example, a $500 annual fee is 1% of a $50,000 portfolio, but only 0.25% on a $200,000 portfolio. Focus instead on the value this fee is adding (and avoid those that don't) and the amount of time, focus and learning you might need to do yourself what the fee is paying for. This is not to say that fees don't matter. They do. Lots. But at this stage the things that matter most are your investments, attitude and decision quality. Fees, taxes and costs will have a much smaller impact on your long-term outcome.

This leads to my ten golden rules of investment:

1. You can choose any two of three factors: the amount you need to save, the return you earn and the timeframe. The third is then determined by the two you choose. Not all combinations are feasible.
2. The selection of product or strategy determines the level of risk and return.
3. In order to achieve a higher return, you need to be comfortable with more risk.
4. Don't take on risk you are not comfortable with, but understand what this will mean for contributions, time and outcome.
5. Any investment that offers high returns without high risk is a mirage.
6. A lower level of contributions will require a longer timeframe or a higher return to achieve the goal.
7. A higher level of contributions will permit a shorter timeframe or a lower return to achieve the goal.
8. The longer the period, the greater the impact returns have on the outcome.
9. The longer the period, the more predictable the end result will be.
10. Shorter periods are inconsistent with higher return choices.

Summary

- Determine whether to pay down your mortgage, invest or contribute to super depending on which is the greatest priority for you: lifetime return, certainty or flexibility.
- If you decide to invest, start with the goal in mind and the date you want to achieve it. For short-term goals, seek certainty. The longer-term the goal is, the greater the proportion of growth assets you should include, focusing mostly on growth assets for very long-term goals.
- The higher the risk you take, the higher the return you should expect to generate. However, there are no absolute certainties. You should be seeking clarity and confidence. Also, don't stress about day-to-day movements.
- There are two types of asset allocation: defensive and growth. Defensive assets have lower, more stable returns, while growth assets have higher expected returns that vary from year to year. Your asset allocation should match your goal.
- The question is not whether you should invest in shares or property, but rather, how much of each.
- Look into debt recycling as a way to save money when investing.
- If you are starting small, use this as an opportunity to determine your reactions to volatility. This will stand you in good stead when you're ready to get serious.

Conclusion

The 8 steps in practice

In personal finance, as with many things in life, the hardest part is to just get started. There are thousands of excuses for not doing anything about it. Believe me, I've heard them all. But don't believe that you need to have lots of money to get started, or you have to get your debts sorted, or you need the next pay rise, or you're doing just fine. None of these are true. Everyone can get more life from the money they have.

If you've read this far, you will know that you can stop getting by and start getting ahead by taking some simple steps, most of which will not impact your ability to spend today. I'm not telling you to give up your morning latte, or shoes, or clothes, or whatever floats your boat. How you spend your money is up to you. I have shown you a system that will help you align that spending with your core values so you will feel better about your money every day.

Don't wait until you have the perfect plan for everything. Just get started.

Helmuth von Moltke, chief of staff of the Prussian army in the 19th century and a renowned military scholar, believed that military strategy had to be constructed as a system of options, because only the beginning of a military operation could be planned. He considered the main task of military leaders to be the extensive preparation for all possible outcomes. His theory is encapsulated in two statements, which translate to, 'No plan of operations extends with certainty beyond the first encounter with the enemy's main strength', and 'Strategy is a system of expedients'.

The eight steps to financial freedom I have outlined take this approach. The steps involve building a foundation from which to grow your financial freedom over time.

Start with the basics of understanding yourself. Search for your core values, which are at the heart of what will make you truly happy. Use this inner knowledge to set some life goals. From these will emerge financial goals that need to be achieved to deliver on those life goals. Only then can you create a truly sustainable spending plan or budget. Finish the foundations by getting your paperwork in order and sorting out your super. Get prepared for the unexpected by building an emergency stash and putting in place the right insurance package (this last bit is the first task that actually needs you to spend money).

Then you can start ticking off your goals: paying down debt, buying your home, investing for the future – whatever is most important to you.

Having read this far, you are well on your way to living the life you want with the money you have. All you have to do now is put the eight steps into practice – and keep practising. In the words of the old Irish proverb, a good start is half the work.

In the words of Johann Wolfgang von Goethe: 'Knowing is not enough, we must apply. Willing is not enough, we must do'.

Finally, let me leave you with my ten commandments to live the life you want with the money you have:

1. Spend less than you earn.
2. You can't out-earn bad spending habits.
3. Just because the bank will lend it to you doesn't mean you can afford to pay it back comfortably.

4. 'Interest-free' isn't really.
5. It's not about the numbers, it's about how you feel.
6. A budget, like a diet, will only feel restrictive if it's not aligned with your values.
7. You can't get rich by cutting out your morning latte.
8. There is no get-rich-quick scheme that's legal and works.
9. Information without motivation is useless.
10. Experiences have a more lasting effect than things.

About the author

Vince is an accountant, financial planner and mortgage broker who founded Life Sherpa®, Australia's most affordable financial advice service. He is a regular guest on the *my millennial money* podcast.

Over a 35-year career in finance, he has seen the life-changing benefits of sound financial advice and is passionate about ensuring that everyone has this opportunity, whatever they earn, own or owe. The techniques outlined in this book are the result of decades of his work developing, testing and applying them.

Born and educated in Ireland, he graduated from Trinity College Dublin into an economy suffering from 12% unemployment and 17% inflation and, like most of his classmates, emigrated – first to the UK and ultimately to Australia. This experience, and the stock market crash of 1987, left a lasting impression and led to a lifetime passion for all things personal finance.

He is the father to an adult son. When not helping people get more life from their money, he enjoys running, cycling and spinning 1970s and 1980s vinyl.

References

Introduction: The latte fallacy

Australian Bureau of Statistics (ABS), *6530.0 – Household Expenditure Survey*, 13 September 2017, <abs.gov.au/statistics/economy/finance/household-expenditure-survey-australia-summary-results/latest-release>.

moneysmart.gov.au, 'What do Australians really spend their money on?', accessed 21 January 2022, <moneysmart.gov.au/australian-spending-habits>.

Reserve Bank of Australia (RBA), *Credit and Charge Cards – Original Series – Aggregate Data – C1.1*, accessed 21 January 2022, <rba.gov.au/statistics/tables/>.

P. Abelson & D. Chung, 'Housing prices in Australia: 1970 to 2003', *Macquarie economics research papers*, no. 9, September 2004.

ABS, *6302.0 – Average Weekly Earnings, Australia, Dec 1979*, 4 March 1980.

ABS, *6401.0 – Consumer Price Index, Dec 1979*, 25 January 1980.

RBA, *Indicator Lending Rates – F5*, accessed 21 January 2022, <rba.gov.au/statistics/tables/>.

ABS, *4130.0 – Housing Occupancy and Costs*, 17 September 2019, <abs.gov.au/statistics/people/housing/housing-occupancy-and-costs/latest-release>.

ABS, *3310.0 – Marriages and Divorces, Australia*, 24 November 2021, <abs.gov.au/statistics/people/people-and-communities/marriages-and-divorces-australia/latest-release>.

ABS, *4235.0 – Qualifications and Work*, 29 September 2020, <abs.gov.au/statistics/people/education/qualifications-and-work/latest-release>.

Australian Institute of Health and Welfare (AIHW), 'Australia's mothers and babies', last updated 15 December 2021, <aihw.gov.au/reports/mothers-babies/australias-mothers-babies/contents/demographics-of-mothers-and-babies/maternal-age>.

ABS, *6238.0 – Retirement and Retirement Intentions, Australia*, 8 May 2020, <abs.gov.au/statistics/labour/employment-and-unemployment/retirement-and-retirement-intentions-australia/latest-release>.

S.S. Iyengar & M.R. Lepper, 'When choice is demotivating: can one desire too much of a good thing?', *Journal of Personality and Social Psychology*, no. 79, vol. 6, 2000, pp. 995–1006.

S.B. Johnson, R.W. Blum & J.N. Giedd, 'Adolescent maturity and the brain: the promise and pitfalls of neuroscience research in adolescent health policy', *Journal of Adolescent Health*, vol. 45, no. 3, September 2009, pp. 216–221.

D.C. Rubin, T.A. Rahhal & L.W. Poon, 'Things learned in early adulthood are remembered best', *Memory & Cognition*, vol. 26, January 1998, pp. 3–19.

C.N. Parkinson, 'Parkinson's law', *The Economist*, 19 November 1955.

S. Stephens-Davidowitz, 'The songs that bind', *The New York Times*, 10 February 2018, <nytimes.com/2018/02/10/opinion/sunday/favorite-songs.html>.

S. Sinek, *Start with Why: How great leaders inspire everyone to take action*, Portfolio, London, 2009.

S.R. Covey, *The 7 Habits of Highly Effective People: Restoring the character ethic*, Simon and Schuster, New York, 1989.

Center for Ethical Leadership, *Self-Guided Core Values Assessment*, 2002 <ethicalleadership.org/uploads/2/6/2/6/26265761/cel_core_values_exercise.pdf>.

Associated Relationship & Marriage Counsellors, 'What Breaks Us Up?', accessed 21 January 2022, <couplecounselling.com.au/what-breaks-us-up/>.

H. Dai, J. Riis & K.L. Milkman, 'The fresh start effect: temporal landmarks motivate aspirational behavior', *Advances in Consumer Research*, vol. 41, 2013, pp. 228–232.

Step 1: Spend less than you earn

E. Warren & A.W. Tyagi, *All Your Worth: The ultimate lifetime money plan*, Free Press, New York, 2005.

D. Ramsey, *The Total Money Makeover: A proven plan for financial fitness*, Thomas Nelson, Nashville, 2003.

S. Pape, *The Barefoot Investor: The only money guide you'll ever need*, John Wiley and Sons Australia, Milton, Queensland, 2017.

G. Ülkümen, M. Thomas & V.G. Morwitz, 'Will I spend more in 12 months or a year? The effect of ease of estimation and confidence on budget estimates', *Journal of Consumer Research*, vol. 35, no. 2, August 2008, pp. 245–256.

Australian Communications and Media Authority, 'Mobile-only Australia: living without a fixed line at home', December 2020, <acma.gov.au/publications/2020-12/report/mobile-only-australia-living-without-fixed-line-home>.

Fight Food Waste Cooperative Research Centre, 'Designing effective interventions to reduce household food waste', accessed 21 January 2022, <fightfoodwastecrc.com.au/project/consumer-attitudes/>.

Foodwise, 'Fast facts on food waste', accessed 21 January 2022, <foodwise.com.au/foodwaste/food-waste-fast-facts/>.

M. Kondo & C. Hirano, *The Life-changing Magic of Tidying Up: The Japanese art of decluttering and organizing*, Ten Speed Press, Berkeley, 2014.

J. Petty, *Start Me Up!*, University of Technology Sydney, 2005.

J. Dixon & J. Nassios, 'FactCheck Q&A: are "almost 60%" of small business owners paid "$50,000 or less"?', *The Conversation*, 14 February 2018, <theconversation.com/factcheck-qanda-are-almost-60-of-small-business-owners-paid-50-000-or-less-91328>.

Step 3: Pay off your debts

D. Gal & B.B. McShane, 'Can small victories help win the war? Evidence from consumer debt management', *Journal of Marketing Research*, vol. 49, no. 4, August 2012, pp. 487–501.

P. Raghubir & J. Srivastava, 'Monopoly money: the effect of payment coupling and form on spending behavior', *Journal of Experimental Psychology: Applied*, vol. 14, no. 3, 2008, pp. 213–225.

H.E. Hershfield, 'The way we spend impacts how we spend', *Psychology Today*, 10 July 2012, <psychologytoday.com/us/blog/the-edge-choice/201207/the-way-we-spend-impacts-how-we-spend>.

P. Chatterjee & R.L. Rose, 'Do payment mechanisms change the way consumers perceive products?', *Journal of Consumer Research*, vol. 38, no. 6, April 2012, pp. 1129–1139.

Step 4: Prepare for the unexpected

Council for Disability Awareness, 'Disability statistics', last updated 30 September 2021, <disabilitycanhappen.org/disability-statistic/>.

Bureau of Infrastructure and Transport Research Economics, *Road trauma Australia 2020 statistical summary*, 31 August 2021 <bitre.gov.au/publications/ongoing/road_deaths_australia_annual_summaries>.

AIHW, 'Cancer in Australia 2021', 1 December 2021, <aihw.gov.au/reports/cancer/cancer-in-australia-2021/summary>.

Mental Health Council of Australia, 'Fact sheet: statistics on mental health', accessed 21 January 2022, <mhaustralia.org/sites/default/files/imported/component/rsfiles/factsheets/statistics_on_mental_health.pdf>.

Guardian Insurance & LearnVest, *Life and Disability Insurance: What 20- and 30-somethings think*, accessed 21 January 2022, <news.guardianlife.com/sites/guardianlife.newshq.businesswire.com/files/research/file/Life_and_Disability_Insurance_What_20-_and_30-Somethings_Think.pdf>.

Step 5: Get the super basics right

Australian Taxation Office (ATO), 'Lost and unclaimed super by postcode', accessed 21 January 2022, <ato.gov.au/about-ato/research-and-statistics/in-detail/super-statistics/super-accounts-data/lost-and-unclaimed-super-by-postcode/>.

ATO, 'Super data: multiple accounts, lost and unclaimed super', accessed 21 January 2022, <ato.gov.au/about-ato/research-and-statistics/in-detail/super-statistics/super-accounts-data/multiple-super-accounts-data/#LostandATOheldsuper>.

Australian Prudential Regulation Authority (APRA), *Heatmap: MySuper Products*, 16 December 2021, <apra.gov.au/sites/default/files/2021-12/MySuper%20Product%20Heatmap%20template.xlsx>.

E. Rapaport, 'Financial services industry opts for secrecy and investors lose out – again: editor's note', *Morningstar*, 20 November 2021, <morningstar.com.au/funds/article/financial-services-industry-opts-for-secrecy/216960>.

Climate Change Litigation Databases, 'McVeigh v. Retail Employees Superannuation Trust', accessed 21 January 2022, <climatecasechart.com/climate-change-litigation/non-us-case/mcveigh-v-retail-employees-superannuation-trust/>.

ABS, *Household Financial Resources*, 30 June 2021, <abs.gov.au/statistics/economy/finance/household-financial-resources/latest-release>.

Step 6: Get your paperwork straight

University of Texas at Austin 2014 Commencement Address – Admiral William H. McRaven, video recording, uploaded 20 May 2014, <youtube.com/watch?v=pxBQLFLei70>.

Step 7: Buy and pay off your home

ATO, 'Individuals statistics', accessed 21 January 2022, <ato.gov.au/About-ATO/Research-and-statistics/In-detail/Taxation-statistics/Taxation-statistics-2018-19/>.

Melbourne Institute, 'Household Expenditure Measure', accessed 21 January 2022, <melbourneinstitute.unimelb.edu.au/publications/social-indicator-reports>.

Foreign Investment Review Board, *Guidance 6: Residential Land*, last updated 9 July 2021, <firb.gov.au/sites/firb.gov.au/files/guidance-notes/GN06_Residentialland_0.pdf>.

Step 8: Invest your surplus

Financial Services Council & Commonwealth Bank, *FSC-CBA Older Workers Report: Results of the National Survey on Attitudes to Older Workers*, accessed 21 January 2022, <commbank.com.au/content/dam/commbank/articles/retirement/FSC_CBA_Older_Workers_Study.pdf>.

N.N. Taleb, *Fooled by Randomness: The hidden role of chance in life and in the markets*, Penguin Press, 2007.

Ray Dalio: If you don't own GOLD you know neither history nor economics, video recording, uploaded 20 September 2020, <youtube.com/watch?v=7Slsh8dLPP8>.

S&P Dow Jones Indices, 'SPIVA®', accessed 21 January 2022, <spglobal.com/spdji/en/research-insights/spiva/>.

References

A. Goyal, S. Wahal & M.D. Yavuz, 'Choosing investment managers', *Swiss Finance Institute Research Paper No. 20–63*, last revised 27 April 2021, <papers.ssrn.com/sol3/papers.cfm?abstract_id=3651476>.

A.L. Evans, 'Portfolio manager ownership and mutual fund performance', *Financial Management*, vol. 37, no. 3, autumn 2008, pp. 513–534.

M. Cremers & A. Petajisto, 'How active is your fund manager? A new measure that predicts performance', *Review of Financial Studies*, vol. 22, no. 9, August 2009, pp. 3329–3365.

Australian Securities Exchange & Russell Investments, *2018 Russell Investments/ASX Long Term Investing Report: The journey matters as much as the destination*, June 2018, <asx.com.au/documents/research/russell-asx-long-term-investing-report-2018.pdf>.

Index

Be better with business books

—————————————

MAJOR STREET

We hope you enjoy reading this book. We'd love you to post a review on social media or your favourite bookseller site. Please include the hashtag #majorstreetpublishing.

Major Street Publishing specialises in business, leadership, personal finance and motivational non-fiction books. If you'd like to receive regular updates about new Major Street books, email info@majorstreet.com.au and ask to be added to our mailing list.

Visit majorstreet.com.au to find out more about our books (print, audio and ebooks) and authors, read reviews and find links to our Your Next Read podcast.

We'd love you to follow us on social media.

in linkedin.com/company/major-street-publishing

f facebook.com/MajorStreetPublishing

⊙ instagram.com/majorstreetpublishing

🐦 @MajorStreetPub